Simply Dedicated

Stories and Devotions From and For Foster and Adoptive Parents

BY

TRACY LOKEN WEBER & FRIENDS

Simply Dedicated: Stories and Devotions From and For Foster and Adoptive Parents

By Tracy Loken Weber & Friends

All rights reserved.

This book may not be reproduced, scanned, or distributed in printed copy or electronic form without prior written permission of the authors.

First Edition: November 2020
Printed in the United States of America

ISBN: 9798671730524

Cover design by Chou Hallegra
Edited by Karen Weber
Published by Grace & Hope Consulting, LLC

Praise for Simply Dedicated

"Foster and adoptive parents are my superheroes! As an educator and a close friend of a foster and adoptive parent, I believe Simply Dedicated is an extremely powerful collaboration of lived-experiences, providing a raw and emotional insight to the daily struggles and triumphs that often go unseen. Simply Dedicated is a must-read for anyone working with children who have faced challenges, especially viewing life from the lens of a foster/adoptive transracial family. I highly recommend adding Simply Dedicated to your book-club must-read list, as it will provide further insight to all faith-based and first responder professionals including school administrators and educational professional development teams working to support children and their parents. Simply Dedicated tugs at your heartstrings, provides an inside view of what life is really like, and will leave you inspired to be the change."

Traci Vaughn, M.Ed., Educator

"These stories of personal triumph, joy, challenge, and trauma reflect the challenges and joys in the journey of adoptive parents. Each day leaves a parent with more questions than the day before, but also more love and gratitude. Sharing the journey with others through heartfelt stories in Simply Dedicated is a needed tribute to those who've chosen to love so deeply, it hurts sometimes."

Danielle Bosanec, PhD

"I appreciate the layout of Simply Dedicated. Each section is a tiny piece of humanity served with hope, love, and a prayer for daily peace of mind. Parents who want to feel the community and love behind fostering, God, and life, should invest in this book."

Madeline Carrera, PhD

"This work – a collection of stories, experiences, and philosophies – from and for those who have dedicated their lives to helping the most vulnerable of our children, is both inspirational and practical. We who help these incredible parents navigate just one small part of a much larger ocean of complexities that surround the children in their care, are well-advised to read some of these accounts to be reminded of the 24/7 nature of their work…and their resilient love."

William Seymour, Ph.D. Licensed Psychologist

"I just LOVE Simply Dedicated! Authentic testimonials are so effective!"

Pattie Godsell, Wisconsin Adoption & Permanency Support Program

" Simply Dedicated is a book that provides transformative insight, words of understanding, and hope for persons immersed in supporting children from hard places. The authors provide a raw insight to their lived experiences, as each chapter presents a personal narrative, moving reflections, and suggestions for solutions for parents, social service professionals, educators, family, and human services staff, and other individuals who could benefit from *learning about the intense and overwhelming life experienced by children of trauma and those who surround them. The reader could turn to a topic that may address their current situation, or read the text as a whole to expand their sensitivity and knowledge of trauma. These chapters provide hope, focus on an individual's ability to thrive, and inspire professionals to gain a clearer understanding of home life. The appreciation for the pervasive and often lifetime influencing impact of trauma events on trauma victims comes alive page-by-page. For professionals providing instruction and training for beginning and in-service teachers, the combination of authentic scenarios followed by guiding questions, Simply Dedicated offers a powerful resource and tool that can be used to expand the skills and knowledge of beginning to understand children who are coming from hard places and have experienced adverse childhood experiences and trauma. The format of the book is designed to illustrate the overwhelming sense of joy and unique accomplishment felt by individuals who see the sparkle return to a child's eye or the aha look of a student who "finally gets it". While in the same story, the reader also gets a glimpse into the challenging road faced by children, parents, and professionals who form the circle of care around each child coming from hard places. Each chapter contains reflection questions encouraging dialog between caregivers and service providers. Finally, the insertion of spiritual readings and insights serves as a source of help and hope for the reader. Simply Dedicated is a page-turner and a must-read by all first responders, pre-service and professional educators, physicians, caregivers, early childhood, and faith-based communities."*

Kathryn Smith, Ph.D., Professor Emeritus, University of Minnesota-Bemidji

"For those who ground themselves and their dedication to foster and adoptive children in their Christian faith, this book of reflections accompanied by Bible

verses and prayers offers insights into inspiring faith journeys that rely on God's love for the extreme strength it takes to parent children who have experienced trauma and need an adult to stand by them so they can heal. For some, the new perspectives on the daily tribulations of supporting these challenging, yet deserving and ultimately loving children, will bring new strength and healing. With more than 20 years of listening to foster and adoptive parents tell their stories of challenge and triumph in supporting children to wholeness, I can affirm that the reflections in Simply Dedicated ring true and will offer comfort to those in the midst of the journey. I can imagine many keeping this book at their bedside to find the strength to carry on the next day and to relish in the joyful times on the horizon."

Linda Hall, Former Executive Director of the Wisconsin Association of Family and Children's Agencies

"Simply Dedicated is an exceptional collection of real-life stories and experiences from families who have embraced the blessings and challenges of opening their homes and hearts to children from hard places. This collection serves as an excellent resource for parents, caregivers, teachers, ministry workers, and community leaders. Readers get a glimpse of the struggles and triumphs faced by foster and adoptive families. The devotional thought that accompanies each story offers the blessing of spiritual encouragement."

Pastor Steven Wagenknecht, Abiding Savior Lutheran Church, Weslaco, TX; South Central District WELS Special Ministries Coordinator

"Simply Dedicated is one of those books that should be required for future social workers, child, and family therapists, and other mental health *professionals. This book is amazing at giving you a real, honest, and personal glimpse into the lives of the families and children that we often only get a short assessment or rough draft of their lives. Simply Dedicated dives deeper into their lives, giving you an unedited, real, and emotional look into the whole child and family system that these parents try to navigate. As a mental health therapist, I often enter clients' lives with the perspective of: "How can I meet them where they are at?" And "What impact am I going to have on their life because my experiences will shape my therapeutic experience with them." This book leaves an impact on your heart and how you view the parents, kids, and family system as it relates to your role and impact in their lives. Even if for a moment, you can leave a lasting impression! God calls on us in ways that we may not know how or why we are called, but we are chosen and we have a huge purpose. We often do not realize the impact we make on the lives of the families we interact with, but we do leave a lasting impression on their lives. Simply Dedicated is more than a book about experiences, it is a glimpse into the lives of families who are strong, parents who are determined to provide for their children, and children who are resilient and have unimaginable strength to overcome the adversity they face from a system that doesn't fully understand their needs and ways to support them."*

Latoyia Webb, ICT Child, and Family Therapist,

DISCLAIMER AND LEGAL NOTICES

The purchaser or reader of this publication assumes responsibility for the use of these materials and information within its content. This information is not intended to be construed for legal or medical advice, nor may it be considered as such. Opinions contained within are those of the author alone and are not reflective of any organization or entity that she represents.

The Authors and Publisher specifically disclaim any liability, loss, or risk, including financial, personal, professional, or otherwise that is incurred as a consequence, directly or indirectly, from the use and/or application of any of the contents found within this book.

Table of Contents

Simply Dedicated 1
Praise for Simply Dedicated 3
Dedication 1
1. Simply Advocate 4
2. Simply Attached 12
3. Simply Awakened 18
4. Simply Awkward 21
5. Simply A "Godincidence" 26
6. Simply A Global Pandemic: Shelter In Place The Next 30 Days .. 34
7. Simply A Hidden Disability 38
8. Simply a Mother's Love 42
9. Simply A Parent 48
10. Simply A Whole New World 54
11. Simply Behind the Scenes 58
12. Simply Broken 62
13. Simply Changed 66
14. Simply Chosen 73
15. Simply Chosen by Him and For His Glory 79
16. Simply Enough 88
17. Simply Family 91
18. Simply Final 94
19. Simply Forever Changed 99

20. Simply Free 106
21. Simply Grieving 110
22. Simply Honest 115
23. Simply Humble 121
24.. Simply Hungry 125
25. Simply Insane 131
26. Simply Inspired 142
27. Simply Joyful, even when everyone is puking around you! 149
28. Simply Labeled Wrong 153
29 Simply Looks Different 159
30. Simply Loved 165
31. Simply Messes, Memories and Mermaids 167
32. Simply More to Love 171
33. Simply Moving Mountains Through Faith in God 176
34. Simply Opening Your Heart to a Child's Family 180
35. Simply Paperwork 183
36. Simply A Parent 189
37. Simply Planned 195
38. Simply Pooped 204
39. Simply Practice Self-Care 209
40. Simply Prepared 216
41. Simply Reunited 221
42. Simply Rooted 226
43. Simply Sad 230
44. Simply Scared 235
45. Simply Showing Love 241
46. Simply Siblings 244
47. Simply Snowed in 249

with a Child-Like Faith 249

48. Simply Teamwork 252

49. Simply Therapy 257

50. Simply Ticking 262

51. Simply Together 265

52. Simply Together Forever 271

53. Simply Unbelievable 277

54. Simply Waiting 282

About The Authors 287

Tracy Loken Weber, M. Ed. 288

Kim S Bushey, A Fellow Handmaiden 290

Erica R. Johnsrud 291

Kirsten Marie Peterson 292

Karen Schlindwein 294

& Amalie Bowling 294

Kevin & Jenny Poston 297

Brenda & Steven Wagenkecht 298

Julie P. Watson 300

Simply Dedicated

Dedication

Simply Dedicated is for the silo-break-downers. It's for the foster and adoptive parents who embrace their inner superheroes to transform the lives of the resilient children placed in their loving care. This book is for individuals who work tirelessly day-in and day-out to traverse complex systems for children in care to receive the health and education services they need.

To those working in the systems, thank you for reading this book. Thank you for helping to ensure all basic and growth/healing needs are being met and for dedicating your life to serve so many precious children. Their futures will be bright because you cared enough to serve, to speak up when needed, and be the voice of change.

Thank you to my new and old friends for believing in this book. To fellow foster and adoptive parents, thank you for joining this project with your fostering and adoptive lived-experiences and stories of personal struggles and triumphs. Your contributions to Simply Dedicated will empower others who have joined the journey of becoming foster and adoptive parents. May we all work to have our stories heard and understood, as well as allow our lived-experiences to work for good so that real system changes can occur. Thank you from

Simply Dedicated

the bottom of my heart for being honest and open to sharing your story and allowing others an inside glimpse into your daily lives.

To you, our dear reader, in the darkest hour, remember that your life has a purpose, your story is important and your dreams do count. You were born to serve in this way. You were born to make an impact. You, yes, you are amazing and an inspiration to the lives you are touching. Keep the faith. Keep showering grace, love, and unconditional understanding to the children in your care.

To my parents, thank you for your unwavering support, love, and grace. Thank you for embracing our parenting journey and loving our children, your adoptive grandbabies, as only a grandparent could do.

To the best husband and father, your unwavering love, patience, and zest for life continue to be a gift to our family every day. Thank you for joining me on this life-transforming journey and for the impact we are making in these lives every day. I couldn't imagine digging for treasure with anyone else.

To my children, thank you for blessing me beyond belief. I am stronger because of you. You are loved to the moon and back!

Simply Dedicated

Download your free copy of Simply Dedicated Coloring Book at http://bit.ly/SimplyDedicatedColoringBook

All of the stories and lived-experiences shared in this book are true. Names and other identifying details of some individuals have been changed to protect their privacy.

Bible Versions Used:

NIV : New International Version
ESV: English Standard Version
GWT: God's Word Translation
NKJV: New King James Version

1. Simply Advocate

By Erica R. Johnsrud

"Speak up for those who cannot speak for themselves, for the rights of all who are destitute. Speak up and judge fairly; defend the rights of the poor and needy."
(Proverbs 31:8-9, NIV).

ADHD. Yes.
Victim of physical abuse. Yes.
Victim of sexual abuse. Yes.
Parent substance abuse. Yes.
Bed wetting. Yes.
Food hoarding. Yes.
Fire starting. No way.
Animal cruelty. Heck no!
Hypervigilance. Yes.
Reactive Attachment Disorder (RAD)...

RAD, that was a hard one to answer—would we adopt a child with RAD? In preparing for adoption, I researched several studies online, read numerous books by professionals, and read personal accounts from adoptive parents. Doing research, my nerdy gift to the world, even counted for our credits we needed to get our foster/adoption license! I read numerous accounts of children with RAD who just didn't ever connect with their adoptive families or anyone, for that matter, a key characteristic of RAD. I'm not sure my heart could take that. I've had a student or two who had the traits of RAD. I felt like a failure because I couldn't seem to connect, and establishing rapport with children was a strength of mine. On the other hand, it is pretty rare to adopt children out of foster care that don't have some sort of attachment issues, but if they were severe enough to secure a diagnosis....

Fetal Alcohol Spectrum Disorders (FASD). Maybe.

We were told in our adoption trainings that the vast majority of the waiting children have an FASD; they fall somewhere on the spectrum, but most likely aren't diagnosed. Our trainers even said to assume they have an FASD! My husband and I teach in an area where prenatal alcohol effects are fairly prevalent. Fetal Alcohol Syndrome (FAS), and the other conditions on the spectrum with ever-changing names are lifelong conditions that encompass so many other conditions. We have a lot of experience, but let's leave this a maybe.

Feeding tubes. No.

We just don't have any experience or expertise with more invasive medical issues.

Physical disabilities-ambulatory. No.

Our current home didn't allow for it without major renovation, including an elevator, and we love having a finished basement. We felt bad marking no, on these last two on the checklist of characteristics of adoptive children that we could handle, but we wanted to be honest and realistic. We have experience with learning disabilities, behavioral, psychological, and mental health concerns, but not the medical ones.

There's going to be a learning curve with whatever children we are going to be blessed with, and we wanted to be ahead of it for our sake and the children's. If we are going to spend a lifetime advocating for our children, we need to be honest and stick to what we have experience with. We didn't want to get so caught up in the excitement of getting one more step closer to finding our children that we weren't really honest about what we think we could handle, what we were skilled at.

Being an adoptive parent of special needs children is not an easy job. We were aware that we would probably be working with several different providers like therapists, psychiatrists for medication management, or perhaps an occupational or speech therapist, or a PCA (Personal Care Attendant). We soon learned that being aware and even prepared didn't quite cover what we were getting into.

During the family medical leave I took before the girls moved in, I spent quite a bit of time establishing providers. There were the usual like a pediatrician, dentist, and eye doctor. Simple, right? No, apparently not all dentists take medical assistance, which is what most children out of foster care will have until they are eighteen or older, even after we can legally put them on our insurance. Luckily there was one dental office in town that took Medical Assistance (MA).

We knew finding a mental health therapist that was a good fit would be a challenge. Cross off any male providers on the list, thanks to a traumatic history. How many providers in rural Minnesota were experienced with the issues related to attachment and adoption? Not many, as it turns out, and the ones who did were mostly full.

We were blessed with the experience we had in attending adoption support groups prior to adopting. One couple said there were not many in the area, but joked that thanks to them and their family, they have "broken one in" and gave us her name. Here lies the next problem. Which girl gets her? We were advised to have different therapists so each one felt safer sharing, since their relationship was strained. In fact, before we were in the picture, there was talk of adopting our girls out separately.

Eventually my checklist looked like this:

- Pediatrician
- Dentist
- 2 mental health therapists
- Psychiatrist for medication management (no pediatric doctors here, but cannot travel that often. The adoption workers preferred an actual psychiatrist)
- Occupational therapist (OT)
- Speech therapist
- Orthodontist (None took MA. Must travel 2.5 hours—our oldest's front teeth were just a few degrees from treatment being a medical necessity. She couldn't close her mouth well to eat or other basic functions, and drooled a lot.)
- CTSS (Children's Therapeutic Skills and Supports) worker
- PCA (waiting list)

- Endocrinologist (our girls were excessively small in stature) travel 2.5 hours to start, but soon would be outreach (doctor will travel to our city).
- Urologist (looks like we'll keep the same one and travel 2.5 hours)
- Gastroendocrinologist (travel 2.5 hours)
- Neurologist (we were told our oldest might be having seizures—travel 3.5 hours)

Wow! We haven't even scheduled appointments yet! We realized years later that we could have had a children's mental health case manager who would coordinate most of this for us. I'll admit, I may have some control issues of my own, and wanted to personally pick out the professionals that worked with our children, but the guidance would have lifted some of the burden.

Another thing we learned along the way was that it was ok to "shop around" for providers (and however awkward it was, or how nice the provider was, I had to remind myself I was advocating for what was best for my child). We made several "returns" (discontinuing some services) that were prompted after a simple question to my daughter from the gastroenterologist, "So what have you been doing for fun this summer?"

Our oldest, who was usually pretty shy, didn't skip a beat, "Appointments. We have lots of appointments."

The doctor laughed, and said, "No really." She nodded her head, and he looked at me. I slowly nodded my head and opened the planner that was sitting on my lap. I felt sick as I paged through each week. We had been a family for only a few months, and this is what my child sees as our life. Appointments. She saw eleven different providers, with a PCA to be added, not to mention the two special education teachers on top of her three fifth-grade teachers.

Something needed to change and fast, if we were ever going to connect and form healthy attachments. We were new to this process, and our adoption wasn't finalized. Quite honestly, I was afraid to talk to the girls' social workers and ask if we can eliminate some of the services. I didn't want to lose them. What if they think we aren't good parents, and decide to recommend that we cannot adopt them? No, we cannot do that to the girls! They have already had a disrupted adoption. On the other hand, what kind of life is one of driving to and waiting for appointments and having workers in and out of our home, if we cannot spend ANY time together and be a family? No, we needed to advocate for the girls and for us as a family.

Our workers completely trusted us and supported us in our decisions. We didn't have a PCA yet for 3.5 hours a day. During the school year, that would be the majority of our time together. Did we really need one? I am their mom—shouldn't I be the one to teach them how to bathe and care for themselves? We can put on bathing suits, and I can teach them step by step how to wash hair and bathe. One off the list, but that service hadn't even started, so that didn't actually help.

CTSS. We already have therapists, and they do some of the same kind of work. We have already discussed how the few CTSS sessions the girls have had were ineffective . They'd spend an hour together, and then each get an hour alone. Usually they were in our kitchen, so I'd hang out and work on some important things in the living room. Yes, that was code for spy on them.

Unfortunately for one daughter, the other had a bubbly and assertive personality and seemed to always get her way: choosing the color game pieces first, going first, and choosing the activity every time, while the other one sat there looking dejected, but wouldn't speak up. Yep, time to let that service go—we needed healthy boundaries to be taught.

Luckily, the gastroenterologist, urologist, and neurologist weren't very often, and weren't really necessary after a follow-up or two, anyway. We got speech services in school, instead of outside. (We probably could have had CTSS and OT in school as well.) After all of that, we still had weekly or bi-weekly therapy appointments, and OT (eventually the girls no longer needed these particular services), and occasional medication management appointments. Whittling down the number of people our girls worked with, while continually seeking the best fit providers (who used the best fit therapy types—there are many besides traditional talk therapy) truly was a big step in the right direction of helping our girls make healthy attachments to us.

Probably the best way you can advocate for your child, especially in school, is to be the expert. The expert of YOUR child. Your child is a whole person and is very complex. Mental health and medical providers, social workers, and school personnel are experts in their field and may have great ideas for accommodations, interventions, and treatment plans, and they can help navigate you through the system, but only you are an expert of your child.

Reflection

"Parents who have children with special needs also have special needs. They need to know more than the average parents. They need to do

more than the average parent. They need more patience than the average parent...and so much more." -unknown

- How would our family bonding and attachment been different if we hadn't stopped some of the services?
- When is the best time to educate others versus just keeping quiet and moving on?
- How important to our child's wellbeing is having providers that are a good fit?

Prayer

Dear Lord, thank you for entrusting these precious children to me. Help me to do right by them in all aspects of life. Please surround me with providers who are knowledgeable and caring, as well as others who "get it". Grant me the strength and patience to interact with others who do not understand the world of special needs and trauma, with grace and love, for they too are fearfully and wonderfully made. In Jesus' name, Amen

2. Simply Attached

By Julie P. Watson

"Beloved, we are God's children now, and what we will be has not yet appeared; but we know that when he appears we shall be like him, because we shall see him as he is."
1 John 3:2 (ESV)

Attachment is critically important for human beings to experience early on. In fact, attachment is most important within the first six months of life. We were taught that children who don't attach to anyone within their first year of life usually have attachment issues going forward. It's an essential nurturing piece, and every human being craves to connect and belong. If you don't attach as an infant, it can possibly be developed, but it's a long, bumpy road to attain.

Attachment is a common problem among adoptive children. It's typical for children not to attach to temporary foster families, especially if they know their time will be limited. Long-term fostering can be hard, as attachment often does take place and causes another devastating loss for the child when that living situation ends. But for adopted children, it's problematic. The desire to adopt and be a family is a wonderful, godly image—it's desired. But, the idea of it versus the reality often looks very different if attachment issues exist.

Our two boys attached to us fairly quickly, even during our time fostering. Our daughter, while very attached to me, was very detached from my husband. Noticing physical similarities between us really helped us bond. My oldest son and I have identical skin tones, and I'll never forget in our first few days together, I pointed it out. I excitedly said, "Look, we have the same skin!" His eyes lit up! He saw it too. After that point, he would bring it up every few days, holding his arm up to mine, repeating my words. He was attaching. We found a visible common trait that immediately helped us form a special bond. Other things we did together helped him attach more strongly to me, but it took him longer to attach to my husband.

Our youngest son was quick to bond. I think he bonded immediately with my husband just because he wanted a daddy so badly! He was also younger. At three-and-a-half, he was easy to rock in my arms and cuddle. Because I was able to stay home with him when he wasn't in preschool, we would sing silly songs and dance around the living room together. We would tickle, cuddle, play games, and simply connect. It took him longer to bond with me, however, because he had been through several foster moms already and wasn't too sure how I would be different. But in the home before ours, there had been no foster dad. He longed for a daddy, and my husband answered the call!

Our daughter was a challenge. While she longed to have a mother who wouldn't leave her, she wanted me, but only on her terms. She had deep and wide walls built up around her heart. She was (still is) very stubborn and determined to get what she wants, when she wants it. She didn't want my husband. Early on she told me she wanted only me, not my husband. You see, she never had a daddy in her life that she could remember, so to her, there was no real need for it. She was going to be a very tough nut to crack, indeed. So, we called in for therapy support!

Just two months after our adoption hearing making us an official family of five, we began Attachment Therapy. At this point, we had clocked nearly 100 hours of various kinds of therapies, and I was pretty "therapied" out! But, hey, you do whatever you have to, right? Well, our therapist was very sweet, but incredibly young (twenty-something). She had no children of her own, and had only been doing this job a couple of years. I wondered if she could really understand, let alone instruct us how to move ahead in this complicated relationship. We began, quite possibly, the weirdest therapy I have ever experienced.

The first few exercises weren't so bad. We had to re-write personal narratives for our daughter to replace what she didn't have with what she now did. But, the last narrative we created was so strange, so awkward, we'll never forget it. They call it a "Claiming Narrative." It was intended to help our daughter see herself in our lives from natural birth on, with us as her biological parents in the scenario. In short, it was supposed to help her see herself as belonging to us. Since we got her at five-and-a-half, we were to rewrite her life from our perspective as her natural parents, from gestation and birth, through every milestone and birthday until she entered our lives.

Once we had this faux beginning written, we then needed to purchase special articles of clothing or toys that she would have received from us during those events. I had to buy baby clothes, a baby blanket, and age-appropriate toys for each birthday, one through five. Lastly, we had to narrate (not read verbatim) this story and perform it for her, all while holding her like an infant (think, holding a seven-year old in your arms as you would a newborn). We had to recall her life story as if from our memories and not our imagination. It was SO hard!

I struggled with it from day one, because I felt the whole thing was one big lie. I felt it was important for her to always remember her real beginnings so she could see the powerful work God had done in her life as she reflected back. My heart was torn! I wanted her to bond with my husband, but at what cost? Of course, we did as we were told, we shared her story, gave her all the things we had bought as we "remembered" each special moment, and loved on her so much she couldn't help but see how much she was wanted!

I cannot say for certain that it worked. It helped, but it also became a problem. Our daughter is a creative child, and she loves to dream and fantasize. This "made-up beginning" began to be requested as a nightly bedtime story. And, while we were told to repeat it to her over and over, by the tenth request I had to have a "reality check" with her. This just wasn't healthy, in my mind.

After reading through it with her one night, I looked her in the eye and said, "Honey, we're happy you love hearing this story we wrote for you, but that's exactly what it is… a made-up story. You know that, right?" She said she did. So, I continued, "I wish this could have been true! I really do! But it's not. And, there's nothing wrong with the beginning you were given. Your circumstances weren't great, but God knew what He was doing. He had us waiting on the sidelines to become your parents. But NEVER forget where you came from! God's glory will be magnified through your testimony by ALL you overcome in this life!" We repeated this to her several times, as the requests for the "made-up beginnings" didn't stop, only slowed down. Within about three months, she finally stopped requesting "her" story. We allowed her to keep a copy, as well as all her "special trinkets," of which she still has most today. But we don't tell the story anymore.

Honestly, we saw the biggest bonding happen when my husband started doing things alone with her; the Father/Daughter Dances changed it most of all! The first one was a bit awkward for her, but now she eagerly counts on these annual traditions. She's gone four times, and next year she wants to attend the Father/Daughter Ball! Oh boy, I think we created a Daddy's Girl! Never fret, God will always show you how to reach your children, no matter what the experts might tell you. Trust Him and you will never be led astray!

Reflection

Attachment to our families is a critical connection. I can't think of a more important attachment than that of a child to a parent. This is why our connection to our Heavenly Father is so important! If we're not connected to Him, then we won't be able to clearly hear His voice or feel His presence as we attempt to work on issues that arise with our kids. We have to continuously be open and receptive to His Spirit, allowing Him to direct us in ways we would not otherwise know to go. But it starts by being attached to Him. We are His, and He is ours, bottom-line.

Prayer

Dear Heavenly Father, my child, [state name], is struggling to attach right now, and I'm not sure how to help her. But, I trust that You know exactly what she needs. Please show me how to connect with her the way I know I am connected to You, Lord. I want her to know that the same parental love You have for us is what I have for her. Help me to be patient in this process. I realize it won't be easy, but I am willing to do what it takes to help her attach. Thank You for hearing my cries, and helping this precious child know how much she is loved and wanted! I love You, Lord. Amen!

3. Simply Awakened

By Tracy Loken Weber

" May integrity and uprightness protect me, because my hope, Lord, is in you."
Psalm 25:21, (NIV)

Have you ever been in a deep sleep, in the middle of a really good dream, and all of a sudden someone is standing next to you? You're in such a deep sleep, that you are dreaming of the largest chocolate cream pie ever, and just as you are about to touch the pie to cut a slice—you are being shaken and hearing, "Mommy—Mommy—Mommy?"

"Mommy, I had the bad dream again" in a trembling voice. Struggling to break yourself away from the largest chocolate cream pie I have ever seen, I awaken to tend to the little voice calling me a name I have always longed to hear: "Mommy." Trembling, she's shaken to the core; she climbs over me and our little dog Charlie within a millisecond, lies in the middle of the bed, covers up, and is shaking with the horror of her past.

In that moment, all I could do was wrap my arm around her and say, "You are safe," "You are loved," and "I won't let anyone hurt you."

That night, her nightmare took her back to before she came to live with us. Back to the abuse and neglect, back to being hurt and not safe.

Trauma comes in all shapes and forms, when you least expect it and especially in the middle of the night. Since 2014, traumatic experiences and flashbacks of the past have caused many disrupted evenings, cancelled playdates, cancelled date nights, and shopping trips ended early with a full cart of groceries left at the store. When trauma calls, the goal is to make the child(ren) feel as safe as possible, no matter how long it takes for them to overcome the episode they are currently reliving. It's hard. Really hard.

It's moments like these that one must hit pause, take a deep breath, and call on God's grace to see us through the storm of their traumatic past. Even after two hours of the worst meltdowns ever, know that God is working, He is working for the good and working through you to heal this child before you. Keep the faith, keep calm, and keep yourself open for those "aha" moments to help your child heal. Listen and hear your children. Meet them where they are. Remind them that they are safe, you are now their beacon of light. Let your light shine brightly as they heal. The chocolate pie can always wait until that next dream, or better yet, pick one up for the family "just because," and celebrate life.

Reflection

- How have you been awakened?
- How has the Spirit helped you to be awakened?
- What do you need to be awakened to?

Prayer

Heavenly Father, we have been woken up; may we have a spiritual awakening in times of distress. During our weak times, please continue to provide us with Your strength to overcome whatever is thrown our way. Give us the patience, understanding, and faith to persevere during the dark times, ability to see the light, and do so with a gracious heart. In Your Son's name I pray, Amen.

4. Simply Awkward

By Julie P. Watson

"And we know that in all things God works for the good of those who love him, who have been called according to his purpose."
Romans 8:28 (NIV)

Awkward. Awkward. The word itself is peculiar, but finding an experience to truly match its strangeness is a bit more difficult. Nonetheless, I think I have one. It was the most awkward experience I've ever had in my life.

It had been a long journey, sixteen and a half years to be exact. We felt like this moment would never come! But here it was. We were about to take the plunge into parenthood! We weren't meeting our children the "normal" way. You know, there was no nine-month period of "getting to know them in the womb" kind-of-thing. We weren't even getting them sequentially. No, no. In all our confidence and wisdom, having faith in what God was directing us to do, we jumped ALL-IN and were about to meet our three children for the very first time!

As we drove up a long, dusty desert road past old railroad tracks in the middle of practically nowhere, my heart raced. We had been given one small picture of these three beautiful kiddos, their brief back-story and the heartbreaking tale of how and why they ended up in the California foster care system. After meeting with their social worker just one week prior, and giving her the introduction picture booklets we had made for each child (a wonderful way to help them better prepare for the initial meeting and transition), we felt ready and excited to meet our future children. We knew we would not just be fostering, but had every intention of adopting them from the get-go. In our minds we were creating a forever family, lovingly crafted by God's perfect hands, implanted into our hearts, but conceived out of His.

With great anticipation, my husband and I finally turned into the long driveway where the children lived…no, where our children lived! It was an old house with a little white gazebo out front, but the "lawn" consisted of dirt, desert foliage, and rocks—the gazebo was its only saving grace—the rest of it looked like an old Western ghost town. There wasn't a blade of grass to be seen for miles. My heart sank for the kids to have to play in such a harsh environment, but they would soon be home with us, playing in our grassy yard.

As we pulled in closer to the house, we could see two small images on the front porch. Our five-year-old daughter-to-be, with straggly blond hair, crooked bangs (we later learned she'd cut them by herself for our meeting), and lovely blue-gray eyes with yellow sunbursts, was standing in front of the porch eagerly awaiting our arrival. She was wearing a darling gold tulle-over-satin dress and silver sandals, and she had a red pocketbook tucked neatly under her right arm. She was smiling from ear to ear. Next to her stood our youngest child. At three and a half, our red-headed, brown-eyed boy with chubby, crimson cheeks was all smiles and hugs—for my husband—but I'll get back to that in a minute.

As we got out of the car, I nervously, excitedly and awkwardly went up to my daughter and said, "Hi! I'm Julie." My palms were sweating. She was gently swinging her body from side-to-side and shyly responded with a very soft-spoken, "Hi." I think that was the first and last time she was ever so quiet or lacking in things to say! I then turned to my soon-to-be son to say hello, but he was already running past me toward my husband with outstretched arms (completely ignoring my existence) yelling, "Daddy!!!" I was a bit hurt...ok, no, it felt like a dagger had just pierced my heart! But as I said, this was an awkward moment for us all, so I sucked it up, smiled, and carried on.

Then they each grabbed our hands and led us into the house to meet their older brother. The moment we opened the door, we watched our brown-haired, blue-eyed five-year-old future son burst into tears, duck behind the couch, then run out of the room as fast as he could. I was a bit shocked at first, but again, we were all feeling quite awkward at this initial meeting. As we ignored the behavior and focused on our two children in front of us, we began chatting, laughing, playing, tickling, and breaking the ice in ways children best understand. The more laughter my oldest son heard, the more interested he became in joining our little group on the living room floor. To our delight, he eventually came out of his room and joined the fun.

We finally introduced ourselves and later learned that people who wear eyeglasses terrify him, due to a previous scary experience he chose not to share. Day one and this was already our first exposure to triggers, but it certainly would not be our last. Children in the foster care system often have triggers relating to their early traumatic experiences. Triggers come out when you least expect them and not all at once. Triggers will continue to expose themselves for years following the trauma.

With a heart of understanding and compassion we loved on our son, hugged and tickled him as he allowed us to, and enjoyed our two-hour introductory meeting. The first twenty minutes were incredibly awkward, but the time, as a whole, was so memorable and joyful because of the bigger picture and why we were even there in the first place. God's purpose was revealed, and our important task was now at hand. Nothing could stop us from the journey ahead—not even an awkward first meeting!

Reflection

God often allows us to feel uncomfortable, uneasy, and awkward when He has a bigger purpose at stake to fulfill. If we're too comfortable, we may not be able to understand a situation, person, or experience in a way that brings compassion and understanding to best fulfill the "big picture." God's ways are not our ways. So, in order to be used by Him in powerful ways, we have to be obedient. We have to allow ourselves to feel awkward to get to the real, God-sized task at hand and accomplish all He has set before us.

Prayer

Dear Lord, help me to be obedient to Your will, even when it feels awkward and uncomfortable. You have a bigger purpose and plan than I realize, and I don't want to hinder the greater work You have in store.

Help me to have compassion, understanding, and wisdom for the children in my care. For all they have had to endure in their young lives, please help them find healing, hope, and peace. Thank You for loving them and me, and helping me love them unconditionally through You. You are an awesome and mighty God! I love You! Amen.

5. Simply A "Godincidence"

By Kim S Bushey, A Fellow Handmaiden

"If you love me, you will obey my commands"
(John 14:15 GWT)

"It's such a coincidence!" We have all heard that many times, but I say, NO, it is a "Godincidence!"

"Cecil, [a girl who my husband's parents helped raise] called today and wants to know if you and Chad, (my husband) would be willing to adopt her five children!" my mother-in-law said one morning. At that time, we were caring for my husband's grandmother in her home with an adoptive baby on the way, raising his biological brother, Patience, and our daughter Love, whom I was homeschooling.

The extended family was adamantly opposed to the idea of five more children in Grandma's house even though there was room enough. We still agreed to take the children for the weekend and then decide what to do.

The social workers tried to talk us out of taking the children because of the amount of special care they needed, but we still said we thought we should try it for a weekend before making any decision. We could not have the children where we currently lived so spent money to rent a vacation home for the weekend. We now had our newborn son, Peace, who was one week old, Patience was one year old, and Love was ten years old.

Social workers showed us photos of bruises inflicted by siblings once again to derail the visit, but we still went ahead after more prayer. The workers sent us with about twelve phone numbers to call for emergencies and said WHEN you need us, call and we will come and get them right away. Gosh, that was comforting—not!

As the first day went on, social workers began calling me: "Are you ok?"

"Umm, yes, why?" I asked.

"We were just concerned."

They called most of the weekend over and over, and each time I reassured them we were all doing well. In the end, even though the weekend didn't go badly we decided with all the pressure from outside family and the fact that we committed to care for Grandma, plus the special care the children needed, we would have to say No to adopting this precious group. I'd read a Scripture in Isaiah 61, especially verses 7-9, and I'd really thought we would parent those kiddos. I felt confused, sad, and a little bitter. I felt "disgraced." Why would this opportunity come to us if we could not follow through? Why weren't we being supported? Did we make the wrong decision in saying No?

We had heard later the children had been separated. A year passed, and we had another adoption fall through that left me very heartbroken and weary. It was another whole year before the LORD began to minister to my heart once again to prepare me for more children. I was afraid but decided if I wanted to be like Jesus I must follow regardless of my insecurities, and eventually I began to get excited about the thought of adoption again. I told my husband, "Honey, I think God is telling us we should adopt again." So began the "war."

I did not dare mention I'm certain it's a larger sibling group! I continued to gingerly mention it, but just as the Holy Spirit led, and I asked, "can go to an informational meeting?" My husband a bit begrudgingly consented to the meeting. YAY! I was so excited; in my heart it was already done! My husband had vastly different thoughts, but I did not know that yet. I thought he was hearing from the LORD the same things I was. However, while I was happily making arrangements for a sitter for the children and for my aunt who lives with us, and calling and introducing myself to a social worker we will call Fawn, whom I liked very much, and signing up for the class with her, my husband was angrily "fellowshipping" with God, letting Him know all the reasons this won't work! He was reminding God of our income and telling Him this just would NOT be responsible! "God, You'd have to double my income!"

Is what he yelled in the field one day. I was oblivious to all this

"fellowship."

Then came the night before the informational meeting. Chad came home from work in a very foul mood. I felt bad for him and was inquiring what happened at work—it must have been a rough day. He abruptly said, "I don't want to talk about it!" and walked away. Now I was really concerned; he never answers me like that, so I now know he's had a terrible day and I just try to comfort him the rest of the evening.

By that night at bedtime, he still hadn't talked about his day and I just could not understand—we always talked. We got ready for bed, and I was still waiting to see if he would share, but I got the cold shoulder. Hmm, I prayed, Lord, whatever is wrong? He revealed to me that my husband didn't want to go to the meeting. WHAT? I thought...UGH now I was mad.

I had rearranged schedules, gotten sitters, and registered, now what? So, I asked Chad, hoping maybe I heard God wrong, "Do you not want to go to the meeting?" "NO! I don't want to go!" he forcefully announced. Now I'd love to tell you I had a meek and godly reaction but...I did NOT. I just said, in a not so nice tone, "FINE, I'll cancel all the arrangements I spent days to make!" Our room became silent and stayed that way all night.

I could not understand. "LORD, I prayed desperately, I know I heard You clearly we should adopt again, so now what?? as I cried myself to sleep. The next day I cancelled the sitters I'd arranged, but I just could not bring myself to call Fawn. I was so heartsick, and I didn't want to tell her my husband did under NO circumstances want to come to the meeting that was over an hour away just to hear information about their program of adoption.

The weekend came and went, and my heart ached. I was so sure of what the LORD was telling me I couldn't let go of it. I couldn't talk to Chad again, BUT I knew I could and would fast and pray.

The next day when he came home, I was making dinner. He stormed in the back door and said loudly, "You're fasting, aren't you?" "What? I'm making dinner, what are you talking about?" Is all I could say, knowing for certain God had been working. My husband replied with an angry, "YOU don't fight fair!" Sorry, but that made me laugh. I could not believe he said that. I asked him why he said it, but he wouldn't answer; he only looked at me. We didn't talk about it again. . . because he was still not going to obey the LORD, or so he thought.

Godincidence: The day after fasting

I was driving when I got a call from Fawn. I began to apologize for not being at the meeting, but before I could tell her why, she said, "Oh, that's not why I'm calling." I was so happy to not have to tell her why we were not there. The next thing she said gave me goosebumps.

Fawn had talked to the head person of our county Department of Social Services, Sally (whom we'd never met or even heard of), and my husband and I were recommended to Fawn for an immediate short-term respite that they could find NO placement for. The child just happened to be the oldest of that sibling group of five that we could not take two years earlier. He was almost like a distant nephew to my husband since his parents had helped raise his mother. I was sure Chad would say yes, but I told her I'd have to ask him first and call her back. I know again God was making a way where there seemed to be no way in my husband's heart.

I smiled when I met him in the driveway, and I asked how his day was. He said, "Fine—what's up?" I asked, "If someone called and wanted us to do a short-term respite for Ching, would you be willing?"

He was confused, so I told him the whole thing, and I also told him Fawn said since we'd missed the meeting an hour away she'd do it right in our own home if we'd like. He kind of laughed and shook his head in disbelief. He could no longer ignore the voice of the LORD.

That Godincidence was so amazing to us because he likely would not have agreed to any other child at that time, and having Ching stay with us for a few weeks opened the door for our next home study and our next sibling group of four.

The following week AFTER my husband started the home study, he got hired for a new job. His wages more than tripled! When he told me how much they offered him, I told him it was not for us but for the "children" (plural) the LORD was bringing us, and he agreed.

Praise the LORD for a simple "Godincidence" that changed the course of our lives, the lives of our children, and who knows, maybe, it made a difference right here, right now, in yours.

Reflection

When we got our sibling group of four, it was an incredibly challenging time. We worked at teaching our children about the love of Jesus, and a way to show love to Him was to obey—"If you love me, you will obey my commands" (John 14:15 GWT). We told them God wants you to obey your parents, and He has a promise that comes with this, and this is how we taught these concepts. This was a standard sentence in our home: If you love me, you will obey me.

Our newest children began to see, feel, and know God's love. Don't ever discount those beautiful "Godincidences" in your life — they will forever bring the LORD glory and joy to your own life if we obey Him. We all have a choice of what to do with what He offers us.

Our youngest son, Peace, who was three years old at the time, liked to snuggle, and lying across my lap one early morning, he reached up and gently stroked my cheek. In his most tender little voice, he spoke, looking intently into my

eyes, "Momma, I love you."

Oh, my heart was melting like wax in a hot flame, and swelling with thankful joy and delighted, I replied, "OH, Buddy, I love you too!" Then, he said in his most stern three-year-old voice, "Then you will obey me!" OH! Back to the drawing board!

I had to laugh! I think that's what we do sometimes to our Heavenly Father, though. We think He should obey our wants, desires, timing, our way. But let us never forget Isaiah 55:8-9: "For my thoughts are not your thoughts, neither are your ways my ways," declares the LORD. "As the heavens are higher than the earth, so are My ways higher than your ways and my thoughts than your thoughts." He is so good, let us obey Him!

Remember in the beginning of the testimony I shared being confused about what I thought God said to me in Isaiah 61? Verse 7 says "and everlasting joy will be theirs" — that is our daughter's name, and I only realized it about a year after that sibling group of four had been adopted — and I cried for another "Godincidence". I thanked God for ways and thoughts higher than my own!

- How about you, any thoughts that may need to be surrendered in obedience?

Prayer

Thank You, LORD, for Your ways and Your thoughts toward me. Thank You for Your amazing grace that leads me to godly repentance, so I can live in the freedom You alone can give. Thank You for being my patient Father, for teaching me Your ways. Help me to readily and joyfully obey You. I love you, and I'm so happy You are my Dad. Thank You for all Your promises that are all "Yes and Amen" for Your glory! It's such an honor to be called into this family. Please search me, O God, and know my heart; test me and know my anxious thoughts. See if there is any offensive way in me and lead me in the way everlasting. Thank You. Bless me indeed, I pray. I love You, Father. AMEN.

6. Simply A Global Pandemic: Shelter In Place The Next 30 Days

By Tracy Loken Weber

"Now faith is confidence in what we hope for and assurance about what we do not see. This is what the ancients were commended for. By faith we understand that the universe was formed at God's command, so that what is seen was not made out of what was visible."
Hebrews 11:1-3 (NIV)

Day 10. Another 30 days to go as we hunker down and shelter in place. Forty days and forty nights.

Tuesday, March 23, 2020. My morning: Six phone calls completed for the children, and new to us is now having three teletherapy sessions completed. One more new teletherapy session to go at 2 p.m., and it's only 10:30 a.m. —I feel spent already. Dinner is ready to go, chicken is in the slow cooker, and all is peace and quiet (so far!).

Just like that, we are all in a new "normal" of being home full-time. My husband is now officially working from home in his new makeshift office in the basement. We quickly purchased a refurbished computer and a new laptop due to all homework moving online for our five children, and no, that was not in the budget. Yikes! Education as we know it has changed in a flash as parents across the nation work from home, are homeschooling/distance learning (whatever this learning from home is now called) with email support from teachers, two ten-minute phone calls from each teacher a week, teletherapy sessions replace face-to-face sessions, all while trying desperately to hold on to our careers.

This is a whole new level of stress, anxiety with the uncertainty of what tomorrow may bring. We are safe for now, this silent global pandemic is out there, and it's invisible. Being stressed out, serving in multiple roles, all while trying to stay out of contact with others—because life as we know it, especially right now, is a precious gift.

As I reflect on this unexpected time at home, how wonderful it is to have our health and to have all of us together all the time. What a gift and blessing to create our own learning schedule, outdoor recess when we want, cook together as an entire family, no more running here or there, building memories, and so much more.

For the past five years, I have spent fifteen hours a week facilitating therapy for our children, and now it's about twenty hours a week for all five children. Add in doctors and psychiatry appointments, occupational therapy, home therapy, I've been running for thirty hours a week. Insert in the global pandemic and just like that, all therapeutic services suspend, we are home, no running, no exhaustion, finally a break for us all to breathe and just be. Wow, I am slowly remembering what life was like before the healing journey began, what life was like six years ago.

Now, it's time to just be. Be home. Be fully present. Be mindful.

Right now we are fully rooted at home during this storm. We are rooted in knowing that we are not alone and that God is with us. God is always listening, and we are turning to His Word now more than ever before. We are fully anchored to God and His grace and speaking with Him more every day. Our fears have been cast out as we hold on to weather this storm, this global pandemic.

Our God is faithful. We cannot allow for outside noise, outside circumstances to cause us to waver in our faith in God and His faithfulness to each of us. It's at times like these that we need His grace, His forgiveness, His love more than ever before. Lean in. Trust our God. Focus on hope, on brighter days, and strive to be your best self every single day.

Reflection

- How have you leaned in during uncertain times?
- How did the global pandemic shift your perspective?
- How did the global pandemic change y our family?

Prayer

Heavenly Father, I praise You. I praise You for always being there with me. I have rooted my thoughts, words, and actions with You in mind. Help me weather the storm I am currently in. Be with me now, hear my prayers, anchor my thoughts in Your unwavering grace as I continue to be a rock for my child(ren). Thank You for always being on our healing journey. In Your Son's name I pray, Amen.

7. Simply A Hidden Disability

By Tracy Loken Weber

"Come to me, all you who are weary and burdened, and I will give you rest. Take my yoke upon you and learn from me, for I am gentle and humble in heart, and you will find rest for your souls. For my yoke is easy and my burden is light."
Matthew 11:28-30 (NIV)

Something doesn't seem right; maybe it's because this child is new to your home. This child looks just like any other child, but the behaviors and outbursts come and go for no reason

In a fit of rage, anything can become a weapon. The rational part of the brain just doesn't work.

Going out in public or to church you will notice the glares

as your child is unruly, acting out, swearing, hitting, acting unsafe, not listening .

The judgment, the looks, now more people watching you and talking about you. The child looks normal, but their disabilities are hidden from the naked eye. Yes, even in God's house you are being judged.

Trauma can present like Attention Deficit Hyperactivity Disorder (ADHD). Trauma can be paleness, lethargy, fatigue, poor concentration, and a racing heartbeat. Trauma can be physical, extremely exhausting, emotionally and psychologically. Trauma can be flashbacks, age regressions, trouble relating and/or connecting. Trauma can be physical like headaches, chest pain, nausea, stomach pains. Trauma can be sensitivity to loud noise, smell, touch, change in appetite. Trauma can be hyper-alert to conversations and all activities going on around them.

Many teachers and staff are untrained, with no trauma background and training. Desperately trying everything, yet still in an unknown territory. Those in authority are unable to relate to this mental health and hidden disability.

The numerous meetings, emails, correspondence from parents, doctors, and home therapy. The heeded warnings you've had with school staff go unheard. Many teachers are unprepared, shocked, and even traumatized. Many just want the child to "sit down and shut up," to be seen and not heard.

Then after months of building up, the day comes when the child's mental health needs are not being met again and they explode. The wrath of their mental health needs not being met is let loose; the volcano erupts. This child will run, explode, scream, cry, swear at you, "pushes" your buttons. Classrooms will be torn apart, chairs thrown, or worse, items broken and others hurt.

Teams try seclusion, physical restraints, talking, going for a walk outside, all will not work. Larger class sizes only increase behaviors, no supportive trauma sensitive staff trained to work with this child.

Teachers unprepared, only add fuel to the fire. They care, but have no real understanding, no real lived-experience of living with trauma. School staff not knowing what to do, calling police on your child and district staff for support. They will look at you like a deer in the headlights—saying they've never seen anything like this before. Your response is, "Welcome to my world; I've been battling this for years".

And at that moment, those in authority gain a brief, yet real, glimpse into your life. New policies and procedures will be put into place because of your child. They will never look at you or your family the same again, more judgments continue.

Daily phone calls to parents become the "norm". Early dismissals, suspensions are just a phone call away. It doesn't get easier. The school begins to insulate itself; district staff are brought in for support. The therapies increase, hospitalizations increase, behaviors increase, medications increase

Your life changes, it will never be the same, all because of something that cannot be seen. Travels in your car can become unsafe due to attacks while driving. The vacations of your dreams become the "staycations" of security and safety.

Your family creates a new normal to accommodate the trauma and meet "well-being" needs.

Your life shifts; the journey continues up and down great terrains, friends come and go. A new community of support rallies around you and your family.

God has chosen you for His work here on earth

To care for, to love and to support this broken child before you on their healing journey. This hidden disability does change you and will be the most rewarding experience of your life.

Reflection

- How can I advocate for my child more?
- How can I share the needs of my child with professionals? What does this look like?
- What do I need to do to be more present in my child's everyday life?
- What positives can I share about my child? What is my child good at? How does my child thrive?

Prayer

Heavenly Father, in times of trial, let me lean on You for unwavering grace, peace, love, and understanding. Help me to use my knowledge of my child to advocate fiercely for my child's needs; Guide my thoughts, words, and action. During times of distress pour over me patience and understanding; allow for my entire body to be empowered to understand where my child is coming from; and allow space for healing to occur. In Your Son's name I pray, Amen.

8. Simply a Mother's Love

By Tracy Loken Weber

But the fruit of the Spirit is love, joy, peace, forbearance, kindness, goodness, faithfulness, gentleness, and self-control. Against such things there is no law.
(Galatians 5:22-23, NIV)

How does your mother make you feel loved? Take a minute and reflect on that.

I don't know about you, but now that I'm a mom, it's amazing to sit back and reflect on the personal sacrifices a mother makes for her children. I have been blessed by my mother—she is one amazing human being who has always been there for me. She has taught me so much in my life and every day as we spend time together on the phone. Every day as I listen intently to her, so many more life lessons continue to be learned. Her never-ending love for me has made me want to be the best mother to my children. To be their advocate, support system, and number-one cheerleader.

My mother was a faithful servant at church for many years until she couldn't be anymore. She owned her own business, supported my father's passion for his own business, raised two children, all while overcoming so many life obstacles. She has taught me that if I want to be heard, to speak up and let my voice be heard. She has shown me how to be a strong and independent woman, something that I now pass on to our four amazing daughters. I will always carry forward her words of wisdom that I can be or do anything I want in life. Her positive can-do attitude and will-power to accomplish difficult tasks she took on faithfully. Her faith and love of the Lord is strong, and witnessing this alone has fostered my faith being strong too. Every single day, I pass our love for the Lord on to all of our children through daily prayer, Bible studies, patience, love, and never-ending grace.

Ever since I can remember, I have always wanted my children to know my parents, their grandparents. Even though my parents are over seven hours away, we connect with travels to see them, daily via phone and social media, and sending pictures and cards to brighten their days. Every day my husband and I are reaching out in faith, as an internal calling is summoning us to bring children closer to God's love for them. Our desire to save their little souls and help each child live up to their full potential is what inspires us to move forward. As a husband and wife, we are serving as their beacon of faith, all while helping their hearts and minds heal from the past. We choose willingly to walk into the fire daily for our children as every day is different for children healing from trauma. For to us, it is a privilege to do so, that we were chosen to parent these five amazing blessings. Every day we are quietly reminded by the memories of their past that slowly come to light as their walls protecting their hearts slowly come down.

My mother has taught me the power of forgiveness. Of letting go and letting God tend to the details. She has instilled in me a sense of being the best version of myself in all I say and do. I have learned the power of moving on and allowing the past to be in the past. Her pure mercy and compassion to others I have admired the most. Her unwavering love, spirit, and selflessness I carry with me every day. She has taught me that no matter what, I am precious and worthy of positive thoughts and energy, and that I must never doubt my place in this world, and to always be with God in prayer.

My mother has taught me that beauty is only skin deep. The true beauty lies within our hearts and souls. How we treat others and how we respond to the needs of others is when the real beauty shines through. I have noticed myself using so many of her positive affirmations to our children.

Here are few of my favorites:

You are so smart.

I like how you show your love to your (sister/brother/dad).

I like how you show your love to Charlie and Tay (our dogs) and how gentle you are with them.

You did such a great job cleaning your room today; would you like to play a game or read with me?

You are so brave.

I'm sorry someone hurt you. But know you are strong and what they did to you was wrong.

Simply Dedicated

I love you.

I like how you have learned from your mistakes.

Remember, learning is your superpower.

You are courageous! I love it when you are open to trying new things!

You can learn anything.

These life affirmations and lessons learned at home have become the foundation of my parenting style. The years of professional education courses, classes of Love and Logic, Parent Child Interaction Therapy, ongoing trainings have also prepared us for the foster care and adoption journey. Yet, at the end of the day, seeing my mother's selfless love welcome God's children into the family tree has brought tears to my eyes. She has welcomed all of our children with open arms, loving on them only as a grandmother can: Playing games, always so joyful, baking her delicious cookies, and laughing appreciatively at their stories even when they were not funny. She has been the best grandmother ever to our foster and adoptive children, loving them all unconditionally and always welcoming their hugs.

God grants us healing, as we pray over all children in foster care and those that have been adopted. May we continue to serve and be a change agent for so many children needing a loving home to care for and support them. May we encourage others to open up their homes to support children who desperately want safety, a home, and to be loved. Let us all continue to support adoptive families and their children post-adoption, for as many of us know that once children are adopted, the real work and healing truly begins. We continue to pray for normalcy, healing, and spiritual guidance to be with us daily.

We know that this season of life is just one small moment in time. One season, one chapter in the greater story of our entire lives. We are trusting God even when we can't see the light and especially when we cannot understand what is happening during the healing process. We rely on our amazing team of medical and mental professionals to guide us through the health and healing processes as we all prayerfully move forward.

Today, my dear mother is in hospice care. As I prepare to say Goodbye for now to my mom, I cherish every day, every single moment I have with her, just as I have learned to carve our special moments of time with each one of our children. I listen with a new ear to every word she says and finely tune in to our children when they speak. I create more time and space just to be with her even if it's just a quick minute, because she's so very tired now, and cherish the special moments with our own children more. I bring Jesus into our lives every day and will continue to do so until my last breath. As my mother is preparing to soar with Jesus, I know that her suffering and pain will soon be over and set free. My mother's love is amazing. I have been blessed to have been raised by such a strong woman of faith who continues to give of herself freely. During one of our recent conversations, she shared that when she passes on, "I'm not going anywhere; I will always be here watching over and protecting you."

May we all love the children in our care with an open heart, doing all we can to show our version of a Mother's love to them—an unwavering love that provides comfort, healing, and support to all we come in contact with.

Reflection

- How did my mother show her love for me?
- How can I be more present for the child(ren) in our care?
- What lessons have I learned from my mother?
- What do I need to give up to be right here during this season with my children?

Prayer

Heavenly Father, thank you for the gift of a mother's love. Help me be the best version of myself to the children in our care. Guide my daily interactions with my child(ren), and allow for me to share with them the best part of me. Help me be that memory maker, and draw them all closer to You and Your love for them. Bring us comfort in the healing moments. In Your Son's name, I pray, Amen.

9. Simply A Parent

By Kim S Bushey, A Fellow Handmaiden

"Fear of man will prove to be a snare."

(Proverbs 29:25a NIV)

Self-Control, my daughter, suffers from enuresis. No one told me when we got her. Of course, it did not take long to figure this out. I thought, perhaps, this is a response to all the change that has just happened; it is fear from being in a new place. However, as time went on and many wet beds later, I realized this was more than that, perhaps this was trauma based.

I began to research ways that I could help and that's when I discovered the word enuresis, otherwise known as bedwetting. How could I reassure this precious child that I was there for her and we would get through this? I could tell her that it happens to lots of children and even adults; and I would comfort her and myself.

We always made sure a light was on at night, or more than one, including a night light, a closet light, sometimes the room light itself, and the bathroom light. I checked "lights" off the list of things tried. We got plastic mattress protectors and encouraged some more. We Checked that off the list as well. We bought a special device which is an arm band and a little device that connects to the undergarments to detect any moisture to alarm the child and parent it's time to use the bathroom, because maybe Self-Control is just a very deep sleeper, although I wasn't so sure of that, I could now check that off the "help" list as well. We trained her on how to use the new device, day after day. We got new batteries. We trained again and again on how to use it, getting up night after night to no avail. We checked all of that off the impervious list of "how to help".

After many months that turned into more than a year of nothing helping and a lot of hidden "accidents" later, we had the dreaded talk about "pull-ups" for bedtime. The child was a bit older, so this was not a welcome thought; in her word's "pullups are for babies". While there was as much positive reaffirmation, the pull-ups still ended up wet and hidden in all sorts of places, until I would smell them out of course. It was like a "game" of hide and sniff.

As the years went by, and several mattress sets, stained and smelly carpet and closet floors later, I began to get weary. I was not so sure this was really fear, trauma, deep sleep, or a medical issue. I researched again to reassure myself I could help her through this. It was really an issue and not just laziness, but that is what I thought: maybe just maybe, she just didn't want to get up at night. I had been patient, kind, loving, reassuring, but I had also gotten weary over the years.

My husband and I had to figure out how to put in an egress window on the lower level just so we could add another bedroom. All the girls in the house refused to sleep in the same room with Self-Control because of the issue at hand. There were times over the years when it seemed like we'd "conquered" the trouble, but it came back. It was exhausting. We tried to help our child understand that "bacteria can grow in places from hiding wet garments and sheets."

I felt like we'd tried everything. What was I doing wrong? I read books. I took all the blame because of the times when I felt angry. This all went on for years. We moved to a new house and the problem seemed to disappear altogether; but no, it was just being hidden and my nose began to sniff it out. I had been lied to again and again. The mattress protectors were hidden in the closet under clothes. The pull-ups were in the package unworn. The new carpet was soaked because it had gone through the mattress and the box spring. The lights were on. The alarm had long been forgotten. The bedrooms had to be rearranged again, it never seemed to happen during the night when I was waking myself up to wake her up but, in the morning, and this mom was done.

Just once more I asked Self-Control again, why? This time, however, came the real answer. "I just don't feel like getting up in the morning, I'm tired." I was speechless. I was angry. I knew it. I know without a doubt there are people who really have a medical challenge with enuresis, it's a real thing, however in my spirit for years I thought this "I don't feel like it" was the real problem. BUT, I just could not bring myself to admit it. I was afraid to tell the social worker initially, later I was afraid to tell the doctor. How could I think that she might just be lazy? It was inconceivable.

I was an awful parent for thinking it and I knew it. Now, here she was saying it to my face. We had a little bit of "loud fellowship" that day. We worked on this whole, "I just don't feel like getting up" thing for a while, even months. We had an appointment at the doctor's office sometime later and while there I brought up this "enuresis" trouble we were having at the end of the visit because the doctor had asked if there was anything else we'd like to talk about.

The doctor, being the good physician she is, began to reassure my daughter that lots of people have this trouble and she would eventually outgrow it. Then she asked me if I'd made sure she had a light just in case Self-Control had any issue with fear of the dark. I began the very long litany of measures we've taken over the past five plus years in helping our daughter and then ended with the comments my daughter herself had said when she told me she just didn't feel like getting up. The doctor stopped. Turned to my teen and said in a nice firm voice, "That is your responsibility, you have to get up and use the bathroom."

That was the end of it! All the years, the mattress sets, mattress protectors, the laundry, the moving bedrooms around, the lights, the pull ups, alarms, books, egress window, all of it was done with one simple firm statement from the doctor. She never wet the bed again. I sure was glad I finally told someone even though I may seem like the "bad mom" for thinking such a thing about my child. Lazy.

While this child does have other issues that are complicated and need help, I thought for a long time "enuresis" was not one of them, turns out, I was right.

Reflection

I confided in a godly woman one afternoon some of the troubles burdening my heart. I told her I was "afraid" to just be a parent sometimes. Afraid because of past experiences with social workers, afraid because of lies spoken to people by my own children, afraid of what others would think, afraid of my own failures of attempting to be "the best" parent , just plain afraid I'd never measure up to all I should be. I cried. She replied with the simplest of statements. "Wouldn't it be nice to just parent without fear."

In my heart there was a resounding YES! I let those words sink deep into my soul. I thought about them, scripture came to my mind over and over to back them up. I HAD to parent without fear. I could no longer be snared. My foot had been set free from the trap. I was incredibly grateful for the simple comment of a much younger mom and I applied that wisdom. Yes, I do it wrong sometimes. I yell at my kids. I get tired. I am not always a godly example. I sneak chocolate in my closet. I get weary from doing well and I cry. I need help. I need breaks because I just cannot take it anymore. While I do all this, yet I deeply love my children. I ask for forgiveness. I would NOT want to go through this life without them, ever. I am a parent. I am here, loving, cooking, cleaning, teaching, caring, playing. I am here with them and I choose to do it without fear of what others think.

Are we still "judged" and do people tell us what they think? Sure they do! Will they ever walk in my shoes to see what it is really like? I doubt it, so they can talk all they want because they will be held accountable for every empty word they speak.

"But I tell you that everyone will have to give account on the day of judgment for every empty word they have spoken."
Matthew 12:36 NIV

- How can you parent without fear?
- How would this impact your family?

Prayer

Lord Jesus, thank you for helping me to just be a parent. Thank you for all the opportunities to grow and thank you for heavenly comfort for growing pains, and for chocolate. I love you Lord, and I want to be like you, help me. Please forgive me for having the fear of man. I do not want to be snared by the enemy like that. You are so good and faithful to forgive and I am so thankful I can walk in Your peace. If I am tempted, I know you will always give me a way out; help me to remember to ask for it. I can't do this without you and I certainly don't want to. "Bless the Lord oh my soul and forget not all his benefits" (Psalm 103:2 ESV). AMEN

10. Simply A Whole New World

By Tracy Loken Weber

The light shines in the darkness, and the darkness has not overcome it. (John 1:5, NIV)

Heavenly Father, draw near me now; I call upon You to hold me in these uncertain times.

As I enter our fifth week of social distancing and quarantine, be with me and those I love.

This year, I celebrated Easter at home, live-streaming church,

Social distancing from friends, family, and loved ones.

In the weeks, months, and years ahead,

I know that life as I knew it has been forever changed.

We are living in historical times; may I stay informed and focused;

May I continue to put our relationship with You first, God.

Simply Dedicated

God bless the first responders and critical care workers;

Provide them with the strength, knowledge, and perseverance to carry on.

Please be near the seventeen million unemployed and furloughed employees.

Give them hope, grace, and support to provide for themselves and their loved ones.

God bless teachers as they continue to prepare.

Emergency/virtual/alternative/distance teaching lessons from home.

Guide their lessons, help them focus on what's most important, let them allow grace to parents.

God bless parents as they continue to support their child's learning while working at home.

Pour over all with Your presence and love; grant them humility to seek out support.

Prepare our minds and daily schedules to have time with You, God.

Guide our daily thoughts with positivity, and grant us Your peace;

Help us to remain mindful, to rest and relax.

Create in me a still and gracious heart.

As I'm able, allow me to help those in need.

May I use this time productively, making time for what's important;

Saying no to projects that can wait, saying yes to what matters most;

Sharing my faith and hope to those around me.

May I shift my focus as I seek out clarity and everything comes into perspective.

Life as we knew it is in the past;

Allow for our lives to adjust to a new normal for living.

Help us prepare for re-entry and re-socialization.

Hope will not be cancelled; my love for You, God, is more fervent now.

When I hear Satan calling with fear, anxiety, or nervousness,

I will respond by saying, "Six feet back, Satan!"

For I know I'm being held; I am Your child, God.

We will overcome. Amen.

Reflection

- How has my life changed since safer at home initiatives?
- How have my child's needs changed? What does this look like?
- What positives came out of being safer at home?
- Did our family grow closer together? Closer to God?

Prayer

Heavenly Father, in times of uncertainty, draw me near You. Come into my life and calm me, let me lean on You for unwavering grace, peace, love, and understanding. During times of distress, pour over me patience and understanding; allow for my entire body to be empowered to understand where my child is coming from; and allow space for healing to occur. In Your Son's name I pray, Amen.

11. Simply Behind the Scenes

By Tracy Loken Weber

"And the peace of God, which transcends all understanding, will guard your hearts and your minds in Christ Jesus."
(Philippians 4:7, NIV)

Are you feeling under pressure? Do you feel like you just can't get enough done in one day? Do your days come and go, and you couldn't even get one load of laundry done? Dishes piling up and all you want to do is sit in complete silence and breathe? We have all been there.

I recall having to refill our weekly pill containers for all five children. I have this special bag that I keep them all in so the medications are always safely stored away. One of our respite workers was at our home, and I sat down at the dining room table just as I normally do to stock up the medications for the week. I pulled out five gallon-size bag, one for each child, and began to line up their individual medications for the week. As I looked up, my friend and our respite worker were sitting there looking at me with their eyes wide as saucers. At that moment, I did a reality check. Whoa, this isn't normal—yet this is my normal. I had become so used to doing this, week after week, that all of these multiple (thirty-one) pill bottles had become my new reality.

Then, when I really took a step back to think about the fifteen hours of therapy a week that is compounded by the after therapy at-home outburst, school meetings, occupational therapy, home therapies, meetings with the county—my full-time job quickly became one of stabilizing trauma, educating others on how to work with our children. The art of daily healing and successfully getting through each day with the demands of the academics, diffusing memories of the past through mother/child home sessions, put us into a daily survival mode. Daily survival, daily growth, daily healing. It's a lot to handle. Yet, we wouldn't want it any other way.

The individual growth and healing we are seeing from each child is truly amazing to witness. When friends and family haven't seen the children for awhile, their responses of affirmation quietly tell us we are heading in the right direction. We have been told that for every year of trauma a child endures, it will take at least three years of healing.

The sweet notes from the children stating that I'm the best mother they have ever had because I'm the mother that doesn't hurt them, I'm the one that's always there, I'm the one they can come to no matter what are the little glimmers of hope that keeps me moving forward. Keeps me advocating for their needs, following my gut instincts and doing what is best for my children.

Recently one of our children wrote this to me:

Dear Mom,

Thank you for always believing in me and encouraging me to be my best. Even when I don't believe in myself, you do. Now it's my turn to do the same to you. If I could give you anything in the world, I would give you the ability to see yourself through my eyes. Only then you would realize how special you are to me.

Love, Your Dear Son (age 11)

Day-in and day-out, the struggles are real. Behind closed doors, not everyone will see what you are going through. The quiet moments of filling the weekly pill bottles, therapy appointments, and home therapies all go unnoticed by others. Yet, this is all part of the healing process. Day-in and day-out the healing journey continues. There is a higher calling for you, for caregivers. A calling of ultimate love, understanding, and unwavering faith. Hope for these precious children of God, for their individual futures to be bright, continued healing and for them to one day be healthy contributing members of society.

Completing tasks of laundry, dishes, and daily chores doesn't define you. It will all wait for you to complete it. But right now, in this moment of time, I know that helping five traumatized human beings successfully navigate being homeschooled, the safer-at-home-orders, and yet another trauma like the current global pandemic of 2020, does define who I am.

Reflection

- How can I find peace with all the behind-the-scenes of everyday life?
- How can I advocate for other caregivers?

- How can I support someone in need?

Prayer

Heavenly Father, sometimes in those quiet moments, the behind-the-scenes and daily life moments can be overwhelming. Calm me during these moments, allow for me to be patient and filled with the hope of a brighter tomorrow. I know that I'm making a huge difference in the future of the child(ren) in my care. Allow me to call on You when I'm in need; permit time and space for my own self-care and for others to come alongside me in this parenting journey. Help me use this time for Your will and guide my focus to where it needs to be. In Your Son's name I pray, Amen.

12. Simply Broken

By Tracy Loken Weber

"May your unfailing love be with us, Lord, even as we put our hope in you."
(Psalm 33:22, NIV)

The day I was long awaiting was finally here. After seven months of waiting for our doctor's appointment, we finally had a meeting to go over our youngest daughter's medication needs with a new psychiatrist. Filled with hope, I picked up our sweet daughter from school; we stopped for her favorite lunch, and we headed to her appointment. We laughed, listened to music, and had a really nice time until we were in the waiting room and the doctor came to get us. The psychologist was super nice, she explained everything just so, and I was thinking to myself that this is the day we have been waiting for, and I'm so happy she's our new psychologist. Our discussion began, and within fifteen minutes, the one-hour session took a complete U-turn, and just like that, my hope was shattered.

My child, the reason why I was there and waited seven months for this moment, became manic. She completely lost it—majorly lost it. My daughter hurt me. She threw her boots, books, wooden toy cars, and even a huge wooden dollhouse all at me. She bit me, scratched me, hit me, and head-butted me. It was a complete manic replica of what she does at home, right here as the new psychiatrist witnessed it all. What an introduction, no time like the present for our new doctor to see what we were dealing with on a daily basis. During the manic episode, the doctor said it was time to call for help and for her to go to the hospital.

Security was called to our session, and even after he arrived, my daughter continued to throw everything in the room at me, clawed at me, and even punched me in the face and ruined my glasses. Even security was having difficulty keeping her at arm's bay.

It was awful. It was manic. It was one of the worst manic episodes ever.

As she continued to escalate, I knew that I would not be able to get her to the psychiatric hospital by myself—that we would need a police escort, and my daughter would need to be transported in the back of a squad car. This would be her third time at the psychiatric hospital and her second arrival with the help of police officers.

I had done all I could do. I held on, counted down the days, and thought today is the day for the hope for my daughter. Until I realized, wait—did I hold on too long? Could I have done anything differently? If so, what?

Exhausted, emotional, and beaten up, I felt completely broken.

We arrived at the hospital in separate vehicles. She was admitted. The staff held her back as I left her behind. I held it together, stayed strong, and told her I loved her and that I would see her the next day. I walked out the door, turned the corner, and fell against the wall and cried. I just cried and simply asked God to come and be here, be with the staff, and give us all the strength to get through this trial. Yet, here I am leaving a little six-year-old again and the pain she is feeling as I can hear her screaming, "Mommy, don't leave me" over and over and over again.

Feeling broken, I knew that a new day was here. Two other children needed me to be their mom, to be strong and resilient and to say that their beloved sister was safe and in a good place. They needed me to push through my feelings, because they, too, have been broken, and they, too, have overcome their pain of brokenness. I got up, got ready, and dealt with the hospital social worker, her doctor, an hour-and-a-half family session, school updates, and home therapist update and continued to move forward. For the past is the past, and the future healing of my children's lives depends on my forward motions. This is one small bump, in one moment of time. This is not the time to dwell on what happened to me, but rather how can I help my child through the horrible trauma of her past toward healing, self-awareness, mindfulness, comfort, and love.

Reflection

- How have you been broken?
- How did God's loving arms help you to overcome this feeling and renew your hope?

Prayer

Heavenly Father, we have all been broken in one way or another. During our weak times, please continue to provide us with Your strength to overcome whatever is thrown our way. Give us the patience, understanding, and faith to persevere during the dark times. Give us the ability to see the light and to do so with a gracious heart. In Your Son's name I pray, Amen.

13. Simply Changed

By Tracy Loken Weber

"And He said: "Truly I tell you, unless you change and become like little children, you will never enter the kingdom of heaven." (Matthew 18:3, NIV)

Having a typical child changes you.

But it's much different than the change that happens when you have one or more children with special needs.

There may be no baby or child showers, no meals brought to your home, no real welcome to the family.

Family members and friends who knew you before the birth, fostering, or adoption of your children with special needs will comment on how you have changed.

They will pull away; they don't want to know the details.

And when I think about it, I have changed. I know they are right.

How could I not change? My life view, my expectations, have changed.

The vision of becoming a parent and the future for your children changes. You begin the journey of acceptance of a whole new reality.

You have to adjust your sails to a new "normal" and saying "no" to "normal" activities.

My life will never be the "normal" that I thought it would be.

Now even the word "normal" starts to get on my nerves a bit.

You start celebrating, and I mean really celebrating, milestones that people with typical children take for granted.

A successful outing to get gas and then home.

Or maybe a trip to a local park where no one attacks another and we get home safely.

A trip in the car for their favorite fast-food restaurant and straight back home without an incident.

A peaceful evening without safety concerns.

Celebrating these moments, these mini stepping stones of healing, now this is what success looks like.

We celebrated making it through a one-hour church service without major issues, meltdowns, kicking, or screaming—but please don't ask me what the sermon was about, because I was so focused on keeping the children from exploding I have no clue what the message was today or any given Sunday, yet we were there. We were seen even through the glaring eyes looking at us in God's house; we were definitely seen.

You don't give up on your dreams for your children, but your dreams definitely change.

You try not to compare your children with typical kids but sometimes it's so in-your-face that it's hard not to.

We can't do typical kid things like going to plays, outings, theatre, movies, baseball, and dance classes.

It hurts, you realize that it has to stop, you have to stop comparing your children to others.

It's not fair to your children, and it's not fair to you.

You continue the journey of acceptance of an unknown silence.

Accepting your children just as they are.

They didn't ask to have PTSD; they didn't ask to be neglected or for their trauma. They didn't ask for their health challenges.

They want to be like other children, to have friends, to be "normal," to be invited to birthday parties, to have a party where other children actually show up.

Love and acceptance is all they desire.

Love and acceptance.

You begin to see the beauty in them more than ever before.

Their joy. Their unconditional love. Their perseverance. Their determination. Their resilience.

You start to notice the things they CAN do instead of focusing on what they haven't mastered yet.

You change. Shift happens. Your mindset changes.

The lens you begin to look through changes, your life changes, and the people around you change.

You become a research fanatic, equipping yourself to be the best advocate possible for your child.

Medical terms and educational terms you had never heard before become part of your vocabulary, so much so that these words now become everyday words to you.

You become the "doctor," and the doctor becomes the "patient"; now the doctor is consulting you and listening to your recommendations and agreeing with you.

When you see another parent of a differently abled child you feel drawn to them, when you once would have walked right past without even noticing them.

You know their struggles, and you lean in to see how you can best support their journey.

You use words like "differently abled" instead of "special needs" or "mentally handicapped."

You become "that parent" whose voice wants to be heard and listened to.

"That parent" who was once greeted at school is now ignored.

Simply Dedicated

You become an advocate, change agent, voice for the voiceless.

Even though people have labeled you "too sensitive" about it and told you that you have done all you can to advocate for your child—yet nothing changes for your child until a major incident happens. This was my experience, when an incident caused the school district to call the police on my six-year-old daughter.

You can't help it.

You change.

Your lens changes.

How you see education changes.

And as you become aware of people who are prejudiced against your child, you also become aware of your own prejudices against others.

Your own closed-mindedness comes to light.

You don't want to stay that way.

You turn to a higher power for strength in the darkest hours.

You soften. You begin to see the world through a different viewpoint.

You change. You shift.

Some of your family and friends accept the change.

Some don't.

They distance themselves, they say they care, but really they don't because this "isn't for them," or they make comments to others about you, asking, "What are they trying to prove by adopting these children?"

Maybe they don't know what to say.

Maybe they just can't handle it all.

Whatever the reason, they are no longer around.

You make new friends.

Friends who get it.

Friends who become like family.

Friends who become your lifeline, who you can call to come at a moment's notice,

who sit with you when you cry, or just listen as you vent.

Me?

Yes.

I have changed.

I'm probably a little less flippant, a little more serious.

I find joy in the simple things and beauty in places

I would have never bothered to look before the change.

I avoid words like "tolerance" and embrace words like "acceptance."

I am committed to judge less and forgive more.

These sweet children have changed my life.

Changed my life for the better.

I am simply changed.

Changed.

Reflection

- How have I changed?
- Through what lens do I see through, or how has the way I see things changed?
- What do I need to forget and make peace with?

Prayer

Heavenly Father, I know I have changed. Please shower me with Your grace during uncertain times. Help me be the very best advocate and parent for my child(ren). Show me, guide me, bless me as I work with the teams that support my child(ren). Give me patience to weather the storms of waiting, being on hold, waiting for calls back, dealing with people who just do not understand. Help me find supportive services to help our child(ren) and family.

In Your Son's name I pray, Amen.

14. Simply Chosen

By Karen Schlindwein and Amalie Bowling

"I am the daughter of a King, who is not moved by the world. For my God is with me and goes before me. I do not fear because I am His." — *"Fear not, for I have redeemed you, I have called you by name, you are mine. You are precious and honored in my sight because I love you."*
(Isaiah 41:10, NIV)

Karen: Growing up as an only child, I believe God had already prepared me to open my heart to adoption. My parents wanted to have more children, but that was not in God's plan. So, they chose to give of themselves for several years as foster parents. We had many babies that came into our lives; some for a very short time, most for a few months, and our first for over a year. Our role, as a family, was to nurture them until they would be adopted by a loving family. I was blessed to experience adoption first-hand; God had planted a seed in my life.

Many years later, when my husband and I chose to start a family, a still, small voice told me we would have challenges. At the time, the voice was unclear, and we stepped into a journey where we faced many difficult days. Infertility treatment began, and sheer stubbornness and drive caused us to forge ahead through each month of disappointment more heartbreaking than the previous month, until we finally became pregnant. I was so sure that this baby was going to be the answer to fill my lonely heart; when we miscarried soon after, I thought life couldn't get much worse.

Because adoption was an option we considered, a plea was sent to family and friends asking them to keep us in mind for an adoptive situation they may encounter. Within a few weeks came the call that changed our lives forever. A cousin's close friend, with two children, was ready to deliver her third and didn't feel she could parent the new baby. Within a couple of days, we met, and she immediately chose us to parent her baby. Sixteen days later, we watched our daughter, Amalie, be born into this world; it was the first time I gave pause to God's goodness. There was nothing else that could explain the selfless sacrifice of a wonderful birth mother who placed her baby's needs over her own. The next day, she placed Amalie into our arms and told us to have a good life with her, to love her, and to be her parents.

Two and a half years later, through the selflessness of another birth mother, our son, Joseph, was born into our lives. Our earthly family was complete! And yet, as beautiful as this family was, something was still missing....

Following a job transfer, we joined a Bible study group to meet new friends. It was there that we wrestled with the message of salvation that we heard. When we finally grasped and accepted God's gift of grace, we became believers in Christ. God immediately placed an opportunity in front of me to co-lead an infertility and adoption ministry for several years at our church. It was the first of many opportunities that He would bless me with over the next thirty years.

My children have known about their adoptions since they could understand our voices. They grew up with adoption all around them and did not think of themselves as different. We taught them early on that they were chosen twice—once by us and once by God.

Amalie: Adoption is the way I breathe and think; it is what gets me up in the morning, and it warms my heart. Adoption is all I know, the way I think, and I wouldn't change my story for anything. But God is the sole reason I am here today, in my family, and why I am living.

Growing up, there was never a doubt or hesitation for me that adoption was normal as it was a part of every area in my life. My parents made sure I knew about the wonderful special gift of life that Lois chose for me. Before I could even tie my own shoes, they helped me understand that adoption was special and precious.

The concept of having a birth mom and being adopted into my family has never been difficult for me to grasp. Lois and Ruth (my brother's birth mom) have always been special to our family; they gave us life and then made the difficult choice to entrust our care to our adoptive parents. For this reason, I am so grateful and honored to call myself "adopted."

Though I was very comfortable and open about my adoption, the world around me was not always as open. Of course, there were times I would get weird looks or hear hurtful remarks about how I was "different" or an "outcast." I tried very hard to educate those people about what adoption was to me. I would tell them that my birth mom, Lois, loved me so much that she made a loving choice to give me the best life possible by placing me with my mom and dad. I would tell them that my parents chose to raise me. I was chosen. I am chosen.

Adoption, because of God, is one of the most important things in my life. When people would say I was wrong, crazy, weird, or different I took great offense, especially when people didn't take the time to understand the true love and compassion that was behind the decisions Lois, Ruth, and my parents made. I felt nothing but love growing up as a child; isn't that how you want to feel?

However, my identity is not in being an adoptee; my identity is solely in Jesus Christ. I came into this world, just like everybody else, was raised by loving parents, and am living a full life. All of this was because God placed me inside of Lois, and then she placed me into the arms of my mom and dad.

Because of my journey, it was not surprising that my husband and I chose to foster. My adoption journey has been a foundation that helped us to reach a decision to adopt our four foster children who are now a part of our Forever Family. We now have the joy of teaching them that they are chosen and loved deeply and, more importantly, about the love of Christ. We also founded a non-profit ministry, Chosen, to walk alongside of and support foster and adoptive families in many ways.

Karen: I used to ask God why I couldn't give birth to a baby. I know that if I had the ability to write the story of my life, I wouldn't have come close to what He did. I can't imagine being a mother to any other children, or a grandmother to any other grandchildren. I can't imagine missing each and every opportunity to speak of adoption and help others on their own journey. Chosen has been another part of our story as Amalie and I now have the joy of working together to continue our family legacy by walking with others during their journeys.

Infertility, adoption, and fostering were gifts that God has given to our family. They formed our Forever Family and allowed us to find our faith in Christ. Praise be to God!

Where Journeys Lead

(by Karen Schlindwein)

Your journey led you to nurture a baby inside your womb.

Your love led you to choose another family to provide for its needs and be able to help your dreams for this baby to come true.

Our journey led us to empty arms.

We hoped for the day we would have children to love, to provide for their needs, to be able to dream for them and love them throughout their lives.

It was nothing short of a miracle that caused our journeys to meet.

God wove our lives together so that we could accept the gifts that you gave to us and live out our dreams.

We will be forever grateful for the blessings that your love allowed us.

We will never forget the decision that was made that allowed our dreams to come true.

Reflection

"Chosen" is defined as having been selected as the best or most appropriate. As human beings, we long to belong to something or someone. We long to be part of something bigger than ourselves. God talks many times in the Bible about how He chose us to be part of His family. He adopted us as His own because He loves us. You are loved. You are Chosen by the Creator of the World.

"For He chose us in him before the creation of the world to be holy and blameless in his sight. In love, he predestined us for adoption to sonship through Jesus Christ, in accordance with his pleasure and will—to the praise of his glorious grace, which he has freely given us in the One he loves."
Ephesians 1:4-6

Prayer

Dear God,

Thank You for loving me so much that You chose me to be part of Your family. You call me Your own and I belong with You. In a world that searches for acceptance, I am accepted and loved by You. Thank You for creating me in Your perfect image. You alone are worthy. Amen.

15. Simply Chosen by Him and For His Glory

By Tracy Loken Weber

"For many are invited, but few are chosen."
Matthew 22:14 (NIV)

Everywhere we look, we are seeking to be accepted, to belong, for us to be chosen. But, I wonder what it would be like, feel like, if we already knew with all our hearts that we are already chosen by Christ.

No matter how you look at it, we all at some point in our lives want to be chosen. Do you remember being in elementary gym classes and the coach randomly selects two team captains. Next, one-by-one, the team captains choose their teams, all while you are hoping that you would be chosen next and not the last one picked. No one ever wants to be left out, the last one picked, or forgotten.

Now flash-forward to your first job. Filling out the application forms, submitting your resume, putting on a new outfit to make the best first impression possible. Hoping and praying that you will be the applicant chosen for the position. The interview comes and goes. You send a nice thank you as a follow-up and wait. With no response. Once again, defeat. Or, did you receive a call back, interviewed more, and after months of going back -and -forth, you were chosen?

Every single day we are faced with so many choices. So many, in fact, that would you believe research is saying we make over 35,000 decisions a day? 35,000 choices! From what gas station to fill up your car with gas? What route to take to where you're going? What should I wear today? How about which grocery store will I shop at? And now let's begin to think about all the frozen pizza items to select. What kind of apples am I going to take home today? Or, is it going to be that kind of day where every choice is going to be a bad one? Candy, chips, dips, and more? A small, medium, or large coffee or soda? Should I wear pants, capris, shorts, biker shorts? Skim milk, 2%, or almond milk? The choices are endless. And yet what an amazing world we live in to have the freedom and luxury to make these decisions.

Sometimes in life, our decisions will be those life-changing "Aha!" moments that make us stop and think. From falling in love, moving to a new city, changing careers, and finding a new church family, to being faced with a health scare. These moments, often unseen, can define our next steps, actions, and choices.

I will never forget the moment I was told that I had cancer. In one brief moment on my life journey, my life changed. Being recently engaged, so many thoughts came to mind. Thoughts of "will the man of my dreams still marry me" ? Will I ever be able to have the experience of carrying a child, to give birth, to bond with a precious child that my husband and I created?. This cancer was not by choice. But, my choice to survive and overcome cancer was in my hands. My choices to embrace the five years of healing, to keep moving forward and seek out health, was all mine to overcome as no one else could do it for me. My actions, my behaviors, and my healing were all choices that I had to make.

Even though I was not able to physically have children, my husband and I chose to become foster parents. We chose to seek out reuniting a sibling group, and we chose to adopt through the foster care system. We chose to create a forever family;, we chose love. Little did we know how much these little hearts would change us, how many "Aaha!" moments we would have, and how our lives have forever been changed.

Recently, on a sunny spring morning, it was a great fresh start to the day and a family first. Our three amazing adopted children all kissed me goodbye before they left for school. They all attend three different schools, three different bus pick up times, three hours apart from each other. My ten-year- old son kissed me on the cheek and told me that I was the best mom ever. Our nine-year- old daughter hugged and kissed me goodbye, sneaking a special note in my computer with the most encouraging and heartfelt words. These were followed by a hug and kiss from our seven-year- old daughter, telling me that I am the best mommy she's ever had because I'm the one that never hurts her, how safe she feels, and how much she loves our dance parties.

And just like that, I felt like a huge Mack truck just hit me. The grace of God's love was unfolding before my eyes. The never-ending love and grace coming full-circle. God's love is stirring in their little hearts has put His will into motion is for His will. His purpose was for our married life to be something greater. Greater than "poor me, for not being able to have my own child," but rather "yay, us, for making the choice to reunite a sibling group of three after being separated for two years and providing them a safe, stable, and loving home." Allowing for this sibling group to be baptized in faith, to be siblings living together, to run free and have a care-free youth as they swing and play on the playset in our backyard. To be playful, and have the opportunity to go to summer camps, sit by a camp fire and just be children without all the grownup items to worry about. These precious children of God were chosen just for us.

You see, sometimes when you are not looking, you may just be called to action.

When you listen, truly listen, and take a leap of faith, --- your choices can make a lasting impact.

When was the last time that you stopped to look at the beauty all around you? The beautiful shades of white clouds high up in the sky moving ever so slowly. The prairie grasses swaying in the field with an old majestic oak tree standing so very tall. The tiniest of individual little snowflakes all unique, different and gracefully falling from the sky. How about observing the seasons of change, the leaves altering colors, and beautiful tulips beginning to bloom. As you take in all of these beautiful creations of God, remember when you look in the mirror, you, too, are a creation of His. Made to be just you, beautiful, strong, smart, resilient, and here on this earth to make a lasting impact. Beautiful, God chose you.

Dear Beautiful You:

Simply Dedicated

This is your life, your day, your moment

(your very own life).

Get to know your soul, your inner self, your inner voice.

Dance your dance, bust a move.

Sing your song, loud and proud.

Take charge of your story and be intentional every second of every day .

Love your day, every second, minute, hour.

Let your heavy burdens go, bless and release .

Pray your prayers, pray for others, and pray like a warrior

Pour your heart out to God, He already knows what your heart has on it.

Embrace your blessings, every single one of them.

Kiss your beloveds, daily.

Give thanks in all you do, all you have, all the blessings.

Forgive your mistakes, we all have them.

Forgive your enemies, you know who they are.

Take time to heal your pain, breathe, heal, give yourself time.

Rest your body, your mind, be one with nature, take time for you.

Share your God- given gifts and talents, don't be shy — --- shine bright.

Practice your passions, and share with others.

Find your bliss, and do something you enjoy every day

Live Your Life.

Love Your Life.

Because God has Chosen You.

God has Chosen You.

Beautiful you, just think about it. In this moment in time, you are already chosen. Now, what are you choosing? Are you choosing to make decisions that are God- pleasing? Saying Yes to following God's Word and being open to trusting His timing. Remembering with every choice we make, God has a choice for us with His will, His plan for us.

So, do you need a reboot? Do you feel that you are missing something in your life right now?

Let's pause for a few minutes, take some time to do some soul-searching and personal reflection. Pause and think about this question: What am I really wanting to do that I just keep putting off?

Is it making amends with a friend or family member? Maybe the calling, the internal voice to slow down more and to be present for your family? To turn off that cell phone and be with your family? To get into His Word? To lead a home Bible study? To pray more with your children? To walk in nature more? Remember that you have 35,000 decisions to make a day with over 2,320,000 over your lifetime. With every decision there will always be some form of cause and effect. The choice is yours and only yours to make. Just making one slight adjustment to your daily routine can have a huge lasting impact on your overall perspective on life, attitude, and relationship with God and others.

So, what will you choose? I encourage you to take some time the next few days or hours and create ten to twenty10-20 "I am" or "I will" statements. Statements that you can reflect on every single day. Say these statements out loud. Say them with conviction;, believe within your whole heart in every "I am" or "I will" statement,. All doing so knowing that you are a child of God. You have been chosen to make an everlasting impact for good. To get you started, please read the "I am" and "I will" statements below. It is my hope that you will be inspired to create your own "I am" or "I will" statements.

I Am CHOSEN

I am choosing to be a Child of God.

I am Hopeful for the future.

I am Open to giving and receiving love.

I am a vessel Shining bright like a beacon of God's love to all those I come in contact with.

I am keeping my Eyes on Jesus, being in His Word and showing His grace to others.

I am living my best life Now, being present, and believing in myself.

I Will

I will be open to receive and give love.

I will embrace each day with a new hope of faith, love, and joy.

I will make the most of the time God has given me.

I will take care of myself, allowing time for hydration, rest, and personal care.

I will be mindful of my choices and stay true to who I am.

I will be an influence of change, helping those who need to be lifted up and encouraged.

What you decide to do every day matters. What will your choices be? What will you choose to do? The future is yours;, it's in your hands, God is waiting for you. So boldly go out into the world, be a beacon of light to others, and spread the grace of being chosen in Christ with every single person you come in contact with. For it is through Him, His grace, that you are forgiven, you are set free., You, dear child of God, --- are chosen.

Reflection

- How have I been chosen?
- How did my choice make a difference?
- What choices do I make every day that makes a lasting impact?

Prayer

Heavenly father, I know that You have chosen me for good. I am chosen to work in the hearts of these precious children, and, with Your help, guide them through their healing and walk in faith with them even during the darkest hours. Help me be that ray of light, the beacon of faith shining bright for Your precious children in our care. Help me to see that this time is being used well and that my focus is where it needs to be. In Your Son's name I pray, Amen.

16. Simply Enough

By Tracy Loken Weber

"But now, Lord, what do I look for? My hope is in you." (Psalm 39:7, NIV)

At the end of the day, all any person desires to know is that they, no matter who they are, are enough. They are loved no matter what. Enough. They are enough.

When was the last time you stopped to really look—to really listen—to really breathe? To know that you are enough?

Is that moment right now? If so, I encourage you to take this moment to be simply enough and to stop—look—listen, and take three cleansing breaths.

Life at times comes at us from so many different directions, all at the same time. For instance, right now I am gearing up for a doctoral weekend of classes for three straight days. As I sit here waiting for class, I am reflecting on a two-and-a-half hour home therapy session that happened yesterday. The therapy ran over by one and a half hours—that's how intense the session was.

Our child lost it. I was hit, bit, sworn at, punched, and had items thrown at me, all while two home therapists saw our child dissociate, go into post-traumatic stress disorder meltdown, and terrorize the home. It was awful. They just watched. They did nothing. I had had enough, and all the while the therapists' encouraging words to keep going, hang in there, you are doing all the right things, was what I needed to hear to outlast this emotional traumatic meltdown. After our daughter calmed down, the two home therapists left. I watched them out the front window as they both turned to each other and said, "Wow!" Wow, right-on! Finally, finally they have witnessed her manic episodes in person. But why didn't they step in to help? Yes, their encouraging words were great to hear, but this was the first time she completely went manic in front of them and they both froze. They didn't know what to do or how to respond. This is when I knew we needed more help, more expertise, more people to come into our healing journey.

Yet, here I am, responding and doing my best to help my child with two professional therapists watching us the entire time.

I don't know about you, but sometimes, as a special needs mom, I have felt depressed, down in the dumps, underappreciated, misunderstood, and a victim of abuse from our child—the child we chose to adopt—the child I love just as Jesus loves me.

It's at these times I turn myself over to God and ask for His loving arms to wrap around our family, and in that moment an inner strength overcomes me. A cool calmness takes over my body and a deeper love, a love I never even knew I had, whispers, "You are enough. You are exactly what this child needs. Right now, know your child needs you; you are enough. Even though you may be feeling broken, you are stronger than you know. Remember it's not selfish to take time for self-care. You are enough…keep going…"

Always know…no matter what—you are enough.

Reflection

- How have you been broken?
- What are three things that validate you are enough?
- How did God's loving arms help you to overcome this feeling of inadequacy and renew your hope?
- What self-care do I need to do for me?

Prayer

Heavenly Father, we have all been broken in one way or another. During our weak times, please continue to provide us with Your strength to overcome whatever is thrown our way. Give us the patience, understanding, and faith to persevere during the dark times, and the ability to see the light and to do so with a gracious heart. In Your Son's name I pray, Amen.

17. Simply Family

By Amy W.

"But when the fullness of time had come, God sent forth His son, born of woman, born under the law, to redeem those who were under the law, so that we might receive adoption as sons."

(Galatians 4:4-5, ESV)

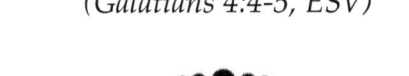

I love going to church on Sunday, but there's one day of the year I cringe a little: Mother's Day. It was especially difficult while we were agonizing over not having children. During the service one year I was having a really hard time, and at the end a young woman sang a song about trusting God. I felt a little better, feeling not quite so alone. At the end of the service the pastor asked all mothers and expectant mothers to stand. The young soloist stood, and I left church that morning in tears.

Fortunately, some ministers realize that it is a hard day for many and acknowledge the hurt they are feeling, especially painful on this day.

Several years ago we went to church with our children's grandmother on Mother's Day, and once again I found myself tensing. The sermon was from Isaiah 66:7-14, about nursing from the breast, being carried on the hip, bounced on the knees, and being comforted. Although I was now their mother, our children had experienced neglect, and I had not been there to comfort them.

At one point I looked to my right and left. There sat my husband, our three adopted children, and their grandmother, who had adopted their biological father. What a beautiful picture of the grace of God. Other than our children, none of us were related, yet God had brought us together and made us family. Families are not only biological. In fact, we become God's children by adoption. Galatians 4:4-5 says, "But when the fullness of time had come, God sent forth His son, born of woman, born under the law, to redeem those who were under the law, so that we might receive adoption as sons" (ESV). All we have to do is believe we are sinners, that Christ died for our sins, and ask for His forgiveness. When we put our faith in Jesus, we are welcomed into the family of God.

Our daughter is now a senior in high school, and I recently finished putting a slideshow together for her graduation. I still have most of her photos in boxes, waiting to be put into an album, so she has not seen many of them. After she looked through the slideshow, she remarked on how much she looks like her biological mom. She does have the physical characteristics of her birth mom, but hopefully she has nurtured qualities that mirror her Heavenly Father.

Reflection

Teacher Debbie Moon's first graders were discussing a

picture of a family. One little boy in the picture had a different color hair than the other family members. One child suggested that he was adopted. A little girl said, "I know all about adoptions because I was adopted."

"What does it mean to be adopted?" asked another child.

"It means," said the girl, "that you grew in your mommy's heart instead of her tummy."

- How should you live as a child of God, and how can you reflect Him to your child(ren)?

Prayer

Merciful Father, thank You for Your comfort in times of pain. Thank You for the privilege of calling You "Father." Thank You for Your forgiveness and for making me Your child. I want to deepen my relationship with You. Help me to respond as You respond, to discipline as You discipline, and to be a parent to my child, just as You are a Father to me. In Jesus' Name. Amen.

Note: The author name listed for this chapter is a pen name. The author requested to remain anonymous; hence, no bio is listed for this author at the end of the book.

18. Simply Final

By Hannah Farinelli Weber

"Love is patient, love is kind. It does not envy, it does not boast, it is not proud." 1 Corinthians 13:4 (NIV)

I was in and out of foster care since I was about seven. At the age of ten, I was permanently placed in foster care. Initially, my little sister and I were placed in a home with an older couple; however, it was never their intention to adopt us. They were very kind to me and my little sister and made us a part of their family. After seven months, we were looking for a new home. One day our social worker called and said that the state had found a new foster and pre-adoptive home for us with a single woman. After looking at pictures, and one face-to-face visit swimming at a local beach, we were moved.

Jana (not her real name) had short brown hair and occasionally wore glasses. She had blue-green eyes that always shined in the sunlight. Jana was kind at first; she'd take us out for ice cream and to the beach. Emma and I were having fun. For me, it was the first time in a very long time that I was having fun too.. Then, our life began to change very quickly. Jana was quieter, more reserved, and the fun had ended. I found out that she was going on dates, with many random men, which didn't bother me much. I remember seeing pictures of her and this strange man that she had previously dated all around the apartment. He had brown hair and eyes, he wore glasses and was only a couple of inches taller than her.

Overnight, these pictures were all over her apartment. Some featured them kissing, swimming together, and even taking funny pictures together. Jana looked happier in those pictures than she ever had been with us. It was sweet, but why didn't we make her that happy? Slowly the pictures went away and were replaced by pictures of my sister and Jana's parents.

About a year later, we were moving again. This time my sister and I were moving into a house with Jana and her boyfriend, the man in the pictures. What we thought was going to be an extension of our family turned into a nightmare. They argued all of the time. Screaming matches over bills, intimacy, remodeling the house, us, the dogs, over everything you can imagine. It almost seemed that the arguments were all day and all night long. We would fall asleep at night to them screaming and arguing.

Jana liked to put her insecurities on to me; she dictated everything I ate and everything I did. She measured out how much cereal I could eat and even how much milk I could drink. Jana and her boyfriend ate in front of the television, while my sister and I were forced to eat in the kitchen by ourselves. It was like there were two different families living under one roof. My sister and I were just there; we made them look "good" to others.

Eventually, I was cut off from everything. I had no contact with my friends or extended family besides my aunt. I was shut up in my room day after day after day. I became even more depressed than I already was, and started to self-harm. After I couldn't find any more band-aids, I told Jana. She acted nice and hugged me; she then proceeded to take everything out of the bedroom that Emma and I shared. After that everything seemed to go back to normal. I told a few friends about what had happened and continued as if everything was normal. At home, the emotional and mental abuse never stopped. My self-esteem was crushed. Who am I? God, can You hear me? We need help!

We had two dogs whom I loved: a lab mix named Lucy and a blue heeler named Bruce. Bruce took a liking to me right away and was always by my side. When Jana would go on her tirades about my school work, chores, or my mental health, Bruce would get agitated and begin growling at Jana. Sometimes he would lunge at her and try to attack, but her boyfriend wasn't going to let that happen. He'd pick him up by the scruff and throw him to the ground and would beat him in front of me and my sister. Every night before I fell asleep, I'd hear Bruce barking and the sound of yelling and eventually Bruce's whimpering. Where was God during all of this?

As my depression got worse, my friends became more worried about me. I was sent to a behavioral health center without being able to say goodbye to Bruce. The day after I was admitted, they gave Bruce away. During my time in the behavioral health center, I received a call from Jana. During the call, I told them that I was sorry and that I wished I had just killed myself. I remember listening to the arguing on the phone again and eventually Jana's voice over the phone saying "Then do it." I hung up and began crying so hard that I couldn't breathe. I was comforted by another patient at the center and couldn't fall asleep that night. In the morning, I called my on-call social worker, as my assigned social worker was on personal leave. I told her what had happened, and we planned to have a visit to the health center. After a week, she told me she had a new place to stay, but that she couldn't guarantee that my little sister, Emma, would come with me.

I took the chance, I just couldn't go on living like that, and I knew deep in my heart that I had to do whatever it took to get my sister and me out of that toxic home. I moved in with the Webers, and after advocating for my sister to join us, two months later she did and we all became one big happy family. I am not the "parent" anymore. I can be a typical teenager. Now I can have sleepovers, go out with friends, go to the movies, and so much more. For the first time in my life, I can be a "kid." I have really cool clothes that I got to go shopping for. I can eat food whenever I want. I don't have to steal it or beg a neighbor for food. Emma and I have all our needs met, and then some. We are safe and at peace in a loving home.

On December 23, 2019, my sister and I were adopted. We are officially a part of the family forever. We are both safe and loved. We are cared for just as if we were their own children. My sister was six, and I had just turned fourteen years old. It truly was the best Christmas ever. For the first time in my life, I received gifts that I wanted and asked for. This Christmas, I cried because I could feel the love not like in years past. In years past, I cried because I couldn't fee the love of anyone or anything. For the first time in my life, these Christmas gifts showed me that the Weber family truly does love me—so much so that all I could do was cry, being overjoyed with emotions.

After all these years, Emma and I are finally home. We are finally forever wanted and finally adopted. We can now share happy and safe memories with our new and extended forever family. I'm finally home, no more moving. Finally, forever wanted. Finally.

Reflection:

- How can I support an older child in foster care?
- Who needs my help; how can I pray for children in care?

Prayer:

Dear Lord, Please help others to open their homes to sibling groups and older children like me who have a hard time finding their forever homes. All we ask for is patience, love, and understanding. Know we have been through a lot, but also know how much we want to be safe and loved forever no matter what. Give hope to other foster children so they can also find their loving forever homes, and lovingly support all of the foster and adoptive parents who take the time to open up their hearts and their homes to care for so many children. Thank You for Your blessings. Amen.

19. Simply Forever Changed

By Tracy Loken Weber

"As for me, I will always have hope; I will praise you more and more."
(Psalm 71:14, NIV)

As long as I can remember, I have always wanted to adopt a sibling group of children. When cancer came and took away my ability to carry a child, I knew that this internal calling would now be my only option for becoming a mother. Little did I know what the impact of becoming a foster parent and adoptive mother would have on my life, on our marriage, and in the lives of our foster and adopted children.

Just like that, in a flash, we received a phone call for immediate action. "Will you accept a foster placement of a sibling group of three? You have 24 hours to make a decision." We sprang into action, accepted the foster care placement, and within a week, on my fortieth birthday, we welcomed the first and oldest of three children into our home. As we pulled up to pick him up at the tender age of five, this little boy was waiting for us on the front step with one small box and a black garbage bag. His only toy was a football; he had no pajamas and only a few articles of clothing, with one holey pair of shoes.

Even though he was so happy that we actually showed up to see him and pick him up, he had just arrived back from the hospital diagnosed with scarlet fever. The foster family that took care of him didn't want him back in their home, gave him no hugs goodbye—just a wave from the front door and a "good luck." We took his little hand and led him to our car. I began to figure out what scarlet fever was and how to help a child heal from this right away.

Two months later, just two short days before school began, his younger sisters, aged three and four, joined our family. The dream of having children and becoming a family was slowly becoming a reality—little did we know how much hurt had already been done to these precious children.

The honeymoon period of having the children with us began. After two years of being separated, they were now reunited. The luxury of being able to spend all day together, sleep under the same roof, and eat breakfast, lunch, and dinner was a treat. This sibling group of three were inseparable. But then came bedtime. We began with a relaxing lavender essential oils and bath salts bath time, a snack, brushing teeth, story time, a relaxing song, and then hugs and kisses goodnight with a sound machine playing "Spring Peepers" to help them fall asleep.

Once it was time to really relax, a spontaneous rage began, and mania set in. The children were running, jumping, hitting, kicking, and screaming until 2 a.m. The panic, rage, and uncertainty was rampant. That was when we found out that bedtime was when our youngest had been severely abused and neglected.

Over the next few months, the needs of our three foster kids and their mental health continued to unveil themselves like a raw onion. The layers upon layers of neglect and physical abuse began to show its ugly head, and the need for professional help became evident. My husband and I read books, attended classes, sought out professional help for the children, and knew that a lot of grace would be needed to see these precious children through as they healed.

Weekly therapy began for all of the children. Home therapists began to come to our home. When we prepared to move, that triggered our youngest daughter's trauma memories. Memories of her abuse inundated her mind—so much so, that at the age of five she was admitted to a mental health hospital and five more times before she was six-and-a-half years old. The neglect, abuse, and trauma from her biological family and previous foster family were extreme. Her mental health was in jeopardy, and our entire family was being affected.

Soon we realized just how real secondary trauma was; our entire family struggled. We missed her so much, but she was right where she needed to be for weeks and even a full month at a time while the doctors worked to stabilize her mentally. It was during this time that we realized what an emotional toll she was taking on our family. Her manic episodes, unsafe behaviors, and unpredictability were exhausting. Our family used this time for everyone to heal, to have a break, and work with her hospital team to help her heal. We learned that taking care of our personal mental health is something that we all need to do. Personally, I've really had to work through this and have come to realize that self-care isn't selfish. Self-care is necessary and something that I personally have neglected for way too long.

In two years, our daughter has stabilized with medication; one remarkable home therapist; a phenomenal occupational therapist; a committed mental health team; an amazing karate instructor; and a dedicated, committed, and caring teacher. Together, a highly trained team has formed around this child to provide a dedicated healing approach for her early childhood trauma. She has come so far on her healing journey, and I just know with continued prayers, love, and ongoing support, she will overcome the mental health and trauma history she struggles with daily.

Mental health is one of those hidden disabilities. It can be very easily tucked away, and when you least expect it, it rears its ugly head. The flashbacks and the memories of previous abuse can come with a specific song on the radio, a certain smell, change in schedule, uncertainty, or taste in food. The triggers can draw back those memories and emotions.

With the recent safer at home initiatives in March of 2020, a whole new fear has set in. Our children experienced a Post-Traumatic-Stress-Disorder (PTSD) flashback to when they were starving, when they had absolutely nothing, no food, hair full of lice. Additionally, neglect and even the fear of our dying have caused four of our children to have serious verbal attacks, physical hitting, emotional meltdowns, anxiety, distress, and tremendous fear. The hoarding of food, sneaking around and hiding treats, stashing the empty wrappers deep within their drawers, and even throwing them behind canned goods has once again begun. As we know, mental health issues come and go with little to no warning.

Slowly, I knew we had to help ease their fears. We discussed how being home from school for almost a month would help us all be healthy. We discussed good hand-washing practices and how to stay healthy. We showed the kids our pantry, the refrigerators, and the three freezers. We discussed how blessed we are to have so much on hand and that they didn't have to worry about going without. We assured them they would not starve and emphasized that they could not be sneaking food and hiding the wrappers. We had to let them all know that we are all in this together, they are safe, adults are working hard to keep everyone healthy, and we love them all so very much.

After the anger, fear, and worry, the tears began to flow. Sobbing, crying, and yelling, their memories of having nothing from early childhood began to pour out of their little hearts. Once again, they were reassured of all we have and that they were safe. The tears, hugs, and sobbing continued as they relived their horrible trauma and past in my arms. All I could do was to listen, support their emotional state, hold them, and love them unconditionally.

During this pandemic, we quickly had to brace for schedule changes — changes including no therapy, no occupational therapy, no karate, no home therapy, no Big Brother time, no outside help. This is an unprecedented time in our healing journey. The support systems we have spent two years putting into place to help our family's special needs are all on hold as our country weathers this worldly pandemic that has caused our fellow neighbors to set off in panic modes with stockpiling supplies. The store shelves are empty, we are all in a state of uncertainty, futures are unknown, and unpredictability reigns as the news is constantly changing.

Simply Dedicated

This new call for social distancing is our normal. For the past four months, we have been homebound, staying out of restaurants, unable to attend church, community functions, family events, dance classes, gymnastics classes, or to going out to parks, all due to the mental health needs of our children. Now the rest of the world is experiencing something we've been dealing with as our healing journey around mental health continues.

We've had to rethink how we live life and what our children will be able to mentally handle, and we have learned the power of only one activity out of our house and then back home. We have learned the hard way that when we can't control what's happening, we should challenge ourselves to control the way we respond to what's happening. That's where the power is. That's how we keep our family calm and safe.

It's times like these that we all need to be gentle with one another and show compassion, love, and support to those in need. We need to be mindful of our own personal mental health so we can, in turn, support those we love and care for. We need to be productive with the extra time we've been given and focus on what matters right now at this moment in time.

We are all drawing back into our homes and our families, spending time on what matters most: our God, our family, and our health. Together, employers are allowing their teams to work from home; at home working parents are now also becoming teachers and so much more. Yes, indeed, this is a thought-provoking time.

In closure, since day one of beginning the journey of becoming foster parents and now adoptive parents of five amazing children, my husband and I have always said that we are "digging for treasure." Every day, we continue to find little golden nuggets of hope, promise, and healing. Even though navigating the mental health field has had its valleys and peaks, as long as we keep on digging for treasure, we know that the future of these little lives will be filled with so much hope and healing.

Keep on digging for treasure.

Reflection

- How have you been changed?
- How has your family structure changed?
- How do you look at life differently now? More grace? More compassion? Less judgment and more understanding?

Prayer

Heavenly Father, we have all been broken in one way or another. I have been forever changed. During our weak times, please continue to provide me with Your strength to overcome whatever is thrown my way. Give me the patience, understanding, and faith to persevere during the dark times, as well as the ability to see the light and to do so with a gracious heart. In Your Son's name I pray, Amen.

20. Simply Free

By: Kim S Bushey, A Fellow Handmaiden

" Be kind and compassionate to one another, forgiving each other, just as in Christ God forgave you."
(Ephesians 4:32, NIV)

We spoke to our children of God's love and forgiveness toward us and prayed they would understand it in a personal way. After our oldest son, Kindness, who was only eleven at the time, experienced God's love and forgiveness for himself and his world really began to change.

There were still hurts he was working through from his biological family, even more than we had first known about. After the children were adopted, they chose not to have contact with the biological family. We just encouraged them to do what they needed to do to feel safe, but we always spoke of the freedom that comes with forgiving.

After a couple years, our son had an opportunity to put that into action. His biological grandmother's cancer had come back, and she was near death. She was in a nursing home for special care. I spoke tenderly to him and asked if he would like to go to see her. His reply was a staunch "NO". I told him she was extremely ill and may not live, but still he refused. I did not pressure him and did not bring it up again. I did, however, pray.

I did not want him to regret his decision later in life. His biological grandmother had raised him for many of his years, and while it may not have been a perfect situation, I know he will come to appreciate what she did do in the future. He came to me two days later and said, "I had a dream about Ronda, and I think I should go see her and pray with her." I immediately worked on arrangements, and we made the trip the very next day.

As we drove, he was nervous but determined to follow through with his mission. When we arrived, he did not even recognize her because she was so terribly sick and frail. He asked me over and over, and I assured him it was her. I eventually had to even confirm it with a nurse because he was so convinced it could not be the woman he had known. Once he was assured, we woke her, and she was so happy to see him. He immediately knew for sure he was talking to his biological grandmother. He shared why he had come and said he wanted her to have Jesus' love too. We prayed for her at the end of the visit.

When we left, my son had a new sense of freedom that I had not seen in him before. I thanked the LORD my son was able to apply what we had been teaching and modeling for him. The biological grandmother died just two short days later.

My young son experienced a beautiful truth found in Scripture. If, in all his woundedness, he could do it, with God's help, can you?

Reflection

• What values would you like to instill in them?

Remember Mary, what do we think of her? Really, I mean, chosen by GOD! She was the handmaiden of the LORD. She was willing to do whatever He asked. She had such a high calling. OK, so not to take anything away from her, I would just like to say, she was just willing, and God knew she would be. Just like you, she said Yes to motherhood, Yes to whatever came with it. Yes.

So now here we are… we have said Yes to this high calling. Today, at least for me, that looks like get the medicine ready to give baby Goodness and change that night-time diaper, make sure none of the three little boys had an accident in bed last night and that Joy remembers to brush and floss those braces well and feed the cat, Self-control gets up and uses the bathroom and tries to put on a smile, Kindness rolls out bed and gets his math done, and make sure to work with Love to drive safely in the Wisconsin snow. I think I will give that job to Daddy so I can make breakfast. I need to make the appointments for the specialist, oh shoot, I forgot the dryer is broken. Hence the pile of laundry, guess we will have to freeze dry some clothes… call the oldest to check in—forgot my coffee again…it's cold ugh, by the way who broke my favorite coffee cup? Is the therapist coming today? Three birthdays this month, Christmas, where was I?

Yes, you can fill in your own list and check it twice, but here's the point: If we don't raise these precious gifts of God, who will? If we don't seek the Holy Spirit for help to train each of them up in what God has for them in His Kingdom, who will? We MUST listen, we MUST obey, we HAVE to model for them the way to live. As moms, we are, after all,

His handmaidens— Let's live like it, love like it, forgive along the way, and smile while we do it.

Prayer

Good morning, LORD.

It has been crazy busy with all my blessings, and I'm very grateful even though I get cranky sometimes. Help me live a life that looks like You so our children can walk in the freedom only You can give. Forgive my shortcomings and sin and use me in spite of myself to do Your good work in those around me. Thank You for completing the work You began! Jesus, I really want my heart to always be open to Your promptings, because while sometimes they seem like little things, it could always end up being a matter of eternity because I know if I can be faithful with a little, I can be faithful with much. I want to be found faithful, wick trimmed, and ready for more. Thank You, and it's in Your name I pray, Jesus, Amen.

21. Simply Grieving

By: Kim S Bushey, A Fellow Handmaiden

" Let us not become weary in doing good, for at the proper time we will reap a harvest if we do not give up." (Gal. 6:9, NIV)

"My sister is pregnant, and she wants you and Chad to adopt the baby!" I'm happy and stunned for a moment but fear quickly rises up. "Oh, please don't get my hopes up because we've been so hurt before." "Yes," she goes on to say, "We remember when you lost those two little boys and how much you loved them and how terrible it was, my sister would never do that to you guys, that's why we're calling."

My inquiry goes on a bit more and I stay reserved and guarded. I ask, "why didn't your sister Karen call us herself?" Tammy helped me to understand she was not sure if we would say yes or no and was nervous to call but when she was ready, she would call. I told her I would talk to my husband, but I was sure because of who it was he would say yes.

My husband was friends with Karen and Tammy in high school. I went out and bought a "we're having a baby" card and wrapped a tiny outfit. I gave it to my husband that evening and when he opened it, I explained everything that had happened. We were both nervous but still a little excited about the prospect of having a newborn baby to add to our family. The "what if" would have to be silenced.

As time passed, we talked to Karen and our hopes grew and my husband and I were really looking forward to bringing home a new bundle of joy. We began working in the nursery. Karen reassured us often saying things like, "don't be scared, this is your baby." "I want you to be excited, this is your baby." It was like she could hear my fears and was able to put my heart at ease. Eventually, we told our children, our family, and friends and we waited.

The months passed and we were so delighted with anticipation. Karen asked us to come to the ultrasound with her to find out if we were having a boy or a girl. We again asked if she was sure, but she assured us she wanted us there, she said, "so you can see your baby." My heart was soring. I called my dearest friend Christine to see if she could care for Love, Patience and Peace while we went to the appointment over an hour away. She could not watch the children that day but suggested I call her mom Carolyn who we loved as well. Then it was all arranged, Carolyn would stay with our kiddos as long as we needed.

My husband took the time off from work and the much-anticipated day finally arrived and we set out for a memorable day. We chattered all the way to the appointment about our new baby. Hand in hand we walked in and were directed to the ultrasound waiting room. Finally, Tammy came in and said Karen was in the bathroom. Then she said, "She changed her mind." We said, oh, no problem we don't have to be here but then she said,… "no, I mean she changed her mind about the baby, she is going to keep it." WHAT?!

"We wanted to tell you in person."….What! I was in the ultrasound waiting room, I didn't understand! She kept talking but I didn't hear much. I finally heard her say we can still come in to see the baby if we want…what, I have to get out of here fast!

I whisper to my husband – "Please stay here and say all the right things, I just can't right now…" I am trembling. I'm desperately choking back waves of sobbing and groaning as I hurry down the long hall to the door so I can get outside.

I didn't want them to experience my pain on a day they should be joyful. I fell to my knees unable to stand once I got out of the doors. The pain was excruciating. I could hardly breathe. I felt like "my baby" just died… again, and again I cried out.

A gentle touch picked me up and said, "honey let's get you out of the driveway." I made it to my truck and continued weeping. When I got home that day, even though the drive was long, my face showed immense pain and I had to tell our children and Carolyn. Now my daughter was crying, and I cried again. My head was throbbing. My eyes hurt and my heart was in desperate despair. Carolyn said, "You know this is just never a part of adoption you ever see." It touched a deep and profound part of her that day too.

After so many losses and so much pain, I had to once again ask myself, am I fully devoted to this calling, or not? Am I willing to keep carrying this cross, or not? Will I obey, or not? Yes, yes, and yes! I can only do this with Jesus giving me the strength.

It's been years since then, although writing this still made me cry... both Carolyn and Christine have gone to be with the LORD and I deeply grieved those beautiful women as well.

Jesus is close to the broken hearted and He's been faithful to give us many more miracles, turning our mourning into joy and giving us rejoicing in exchange for our deepest sorrows. He's given us not just one more son, but two and three more beautiful daughters… and only He knows if others will join this family He is knitting together in Love. I do know, my arms will always be open.

Reflection

One day, I got a call from an adoption worker. She wanted to know if I would minister to a pastor's wife who had recently been devastated by a "failed adoption." I prayed the LORD would help me, and I met the gentle woman at a coffee shop. She cried as she told me all that had happened. I felt her tears, I understood them. I heard her pain as she explained those who could not understand why she was "so upset because it wasn't really her baby anyway."

I knew this grief all too well. Sitting with her, I just wanted God to use my pain and healing to comfort her. She seemed to feel better just having someone be able to understand but, in the end, she vowed to never try again. It has been a long time since then, and I never forgot her, and I've prayed for her family. My heart broke for them, and I so long to have them comforted and carry the beautiful cross of adoption. I did not give up, and the LORD blessed us with many more children.

> "Trust in the LORD with all your heart, and lean not on your own understanding; in all your ways acknowledge Him and He shall direct your paths."
> (Proverbs 3:5-6 NKJV)

- What will you do with your pain?
- Will you allow the Comforter to be your healer?
- Will you let go and let God?

Prayer

Dear Jesus, hear my heart, take the fear, and cast it out by Your perfect Love. Make me whole in You. I trust You. You are faithful, so here I am, complete the work You began in me! Thank You for Your compassion and storing my tears because they are precious to You. I know You make all things beautiful in Your time. I appreciate You and want to continue in the good works You prepared for me to do. Make me strong for Your tasks. I love You. Amen

22. Simply Honest

By Julie P. Watson

"The Lord detests lying lips, but he delights in people who are trustworthy." (Proverbs 12:22, NIV)

I'm sure you've heard several famous proverbs regarding honesty. "Honesty is the best policy." Or, "the truth will set you free!" Mark Twain's quote, "When in doubt tell the truth," is certainly one I've heard since elementary school. They're easy enough to understand and remember by school age, but only if a child is raised with morals from the beginning. A truthful foundation is a core requirement in becoming a moral, law-abiding citizen.

Kids know how to lie. Lying is easy. Lying is a sin, and we're born into sin. We have to learn to do right and choose to stop doing wrong. But telling the truth is hard when no one has explained why it's important or taught you how to do it.

Simply Dedicated

For children in foster care who have little trust of anyone, and often no moral instruction, being honest is just not important. They are in a constant state of survival while going through the system. There are two ways they survive: fight or flight. In the flight mode, they run away from problems until (hopefully) they learn to cope by facing their problems. In fight mode, they do whatever is necessary to get what they need/want to survive, and lying is step one. They may learn about truth from a foster parent one week, only to be moved into another foster home the next. Moral lessons take repetition and regular modeling to be fully learned and retained. Equally, there needs to be a significant reason why honesty is so important.

In walks trust and integrity—two vital characteristics that no relationship on the planet can withstand if they are absent. They're also the hardest to teach to a child who's been in fight mode for so long they've become a habitual liar. My daughter is such. I can't tell you how many tears I have shed knowing she prefers deception to truth, especially since I am an honesty-loving, truth-telling fiend. I'm very black and white when it comes to truth. There is no gray, and little, white lies don't help anyone. I use the old adage, "If you can't say something nice, don't say anything at all." If people insist on my opinion, they'll always get the truth. I try very hard to say things tactfully, but will not liquify my opinion to spare the truth. This has been a problem for some in the past, but most appreciate my willingness to be honest, even if it's not necessarily what they wanted to hear.

What telling the truth has created is repeated requests for my opinions from friends who trust me, knowing they'll always get the truth. Additionally, I always received outstanding performance reviews pertaining to my trustworthiness and integrity from past employers. It's precisely why I was chosen to become a leader of several organizations. Integrity and trustworthiness are top characteristics desired by employers when hiring new employees—I know, I was in Human Resources for seven years, and it was at the top of every manager's "want list." I have shared many of these related examples with my daughter over the years to explain the importance of honesty and integrity. Even for trust to develop between us I've pleaded with her to be honest, just as I have always been honest with her. Modeling honesty is the best way to teach a child to trust.

I recall one time, after she had lied about something fairly big (there are so many I can't remember specifics anymore), I read some parenting tips online for breaking through this area of concern many parents share. The author said she used this method on her habitually lying child, and it stopped it in her tracks. Out of desperation, I gave it a try. The only problem was, it involved a lie from the parent to show the child how bad it felt to be lied to! Since I had promised my kids from day one that I would never lie to them, I had to go into it a little differently. I warned her, "I promised I would never lie to you, but so that you understand what it feels like, I am going to lie to you one time when you least expect it." She just stared at me blankly with little concern.

This took place about three years into parenting her. The day came that I did what this tip-sharing parent had suggested. Serve up a wonderful cup of ice cream, but sprinkle some salt on top without the child knowing. Once they take their first bite and taste that salt and want to spit it out, you say, "Just like the bad taste you have in your mouth right now, lying leaves a bad taste in your mouth and my heart for days to come. It causes trust to be lost, and not easily regained. The next time you want to lie, remember the bad taste you're experiencing right now." When I gave my daughter the bite (I did not sprinkle the whole cup, just the first bite), I said what I shared above, then added, "Remember, I warned you that one day I would lie to you when you least expect it so you would understand what it feels like to be lied to. Today is that day."

Her response was initially good. At first she didn't even want to finish the rest of her ice cream (after I reassured her it was only the first bite salted, she conceded). I thought it had worked. I used this technique because it involved sweets—something she was seriously addicted to. I knew she wouldn't turn it down, and the physical distaste would be something she would remember for a long time. For three days she didn't lie about a thing. It was amazing! My daughter lied multiple times a day, even about the stupidest things, so for me, I felt as if it was a win. But by day four, she was back at it. Habits die hard. Bad habits die harder.

I definitely don't recommend this technique with foster kids at all. My daughter had been adopted for over a year by this point, and as I said, I was desperate! But it didn't work, and I'll tell you why. Perhaps it worked for that mom, perhaps not. She could have written her success in that three-day window, who knows. But foster kids are so used to people lying to them, they already expect it. They need truth modeled, and even "preparing them for a future lie" isn't a wise decision; it breaks good faith. I have made a ton of parenting mistakes. This one is memorable.

Taking parenting advice from non-foster parents with their own, biological children does not work. You cannot parent foster kids the same way you would your own. There are too many variables, past traumas to factor in, the temporary-ness of your situation, and the fact that they were not necessarily raised with a moral compass. You basically have to start over from the beginning. You have to figuratively strip them down, in order to morally build them back up.

I'll be honest. We saw a lot of wonderful changes happen during fostering, but real, deep-seated change didn't start happening until the kids finally realized they weren't going anywhere. Stability and security attained by being part of a forever family took about six months to a year for them to even start "getting it." The standard rule, as we were taught, goes like this: For every year they're in foster care, it takes two years out of it for them to adjust. My kids have approximately eight and ten years to get "there." We're only four years post-adoption, so we're about halfway. If adoption is your desire, it's a long journey ahead. Make sure you go into it knowing you'll need God-sized patience and grace, but don't forget to give yourself some in the process.

Reflection

Honesty is a godly attribute, and we should not only desire to be truthful, but actually practice it always. Modeling honesty is the best way to teach your child(ren) how to be honest, as well as how to trust others. God knows this is a tough one (we're still working on it). But He will help you to teach your child(ren) with just the right methods. Remember, each child is wired very differently. The way you teach one child may not work for another. Keep plugging away at it—God's cheering you on to victory in Him!

Prayer

Dear Heavenly Father, please help me teach my children to be honest in all areas of their lives. Help them to understand the importance of trust, honesty, and integrity—each one so critical for every relationship they will ever have. Help me to always be honest with them, so they see me modeling Your truths. Thank You for Your grace, and help me to give it in spades! Give me patience and understanding like never before, but above all help me to teach truth in love! In Your Son's precious name. Amen

23. Simply Humble

By Kim S Bushey, A Fellow Handmaiden

" Fools mock at making amends for sin, but goodwill is found among the upright."
(Proverbs 14:9, NIV)

Before we got our sibling group of four, they had been taught to steal and unfortunately become particularly good at it! Even so there were times when they got caught and were eventually banned from entering stores like Wal-Mart, Dollar Store, and Walgreens in their previous hometown, to name a few. They were very scared the first time I took them to the store with me, and they looked around as if they were fugitives.

After living with us and hearing lessons about being responsible for our actions, our daughter, Self-Control, asked if she could write "sorry letters" to the stores which she had stolen from, and if I would take her to each store. I said,

"Absolutely!"

This was a huge breakthrough for this child. Not to mention a great relief for this mother. It took her some time to actually finish those letters, but I never pushed her because I wanted it to come from the sincerity in her own heart. I rested in the thought that God had begun this work in her and He would complete it.

I had an appointment with a specialist for baby Goodness in Self-Control's former hometown, so she came along. I was a bit concerned how she may respond to being in this town and it was indeed proving exceedingly difficult for her. It was bringing back a lot of traumatic memories. I kept checking in with her emotions and trying to support and encourage her.

At the first store, she felt so sick to her stomach because she was so afraid, she thought she may be arrested after confessing to them. Again, I tried to reassure her and even reminded her she was in no way being required to do this, but in her mind, she was willing to face the consequences whatever they may be anyway—she had to make this right. I was so thankful she was feeling this way.

We asked for a manager in each store. Our daughter would explain how she and her siblings used to be taught to steal from this store and how now her new parents don't steal and teach them not to. She told them sometimes she still wants to steal, but she doesn't. Self-Control said, "This is a letter because I want you to know Jesus and to know I'm really sorry I stole from here." We were met with a lot of shocked looks and a lot of support for Self-Control and her biological siblings because of what she was doing. She received praise and a "Welcome back to our store anytime!" in every store we went to. Some of Self-

Control's fears melted away that day and I know she found joy in being responsible for setting things right.

Reflection

> *"His divine power has given us everything we need for life and godliness through our knowledge of him who called us by His own glory and goodness. Through these, he has given us His very great and precious promises, so that through them you may participate in the divine nature and escape the corruption in the world caused by evil desires."*
>
> *(2nd Peter 1: 3-4 NIV)*

Making amends for sin can feel scary. It makes us vulnerable, and sometimes we even feel justified in holding on to an offense. Both of those things are just a trap we need to be set free from.

When I became a Christian, the LORD showed me in His word that I needed to reconcile with my dad. At that time, I hadn't spoken to him in about eight years. He had adopted me when I was in the first grade, but he was the only dad I'd ever known since I was a baby. My mother was young, and I was placed in foster care before she met and married my dad. Afterwards, she was able to bring me back home and I now had a new little sister, my dad's biological child. He struggled to love me as his own and it made for a rough start in life. I thank God for the love of my mom and sister. As I got older, I rebelled against him and was always able to justify it. I had a good reason right!?

But here I was years later, and my Heavenly Father made it noticeably clear that things needed to change if I was to go further in maturing as His child. I obeyed Him, and one afternoon I went to my dad's house and told him I was sorry for all the wrong I had done and that I loved him. I knew what he did or did not do in response would not matter. I had to have my heart right before God. I'm so thankful I obeyed because I had a great relationship for the first time in my life with my dad and he very unexpectedly died just six months later! I have to ask myself, what will God do if I am willing to humble myself today? He will lift me up.

• What may help your kiddo feel better about themselves? Only God knows, so let us ask the question and see how He leads.

Prayer

LORD Jesus, give me the grace to humble myself today. Make me into the mature Christian you died for me to be. I want all of You! Jesus, You are the way, the truth, and the life. I'm coming through You. Thank you for caring for me. Thank you that I can give You any and all anxious thoughts and You will guard my heart and mind, give me peace and set me free! AMEN

24.. Simply Hungry

By Julie P. Watson

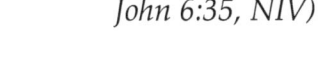

"Then Jesus declared, 'I am the bread of life. Whoever comes to me will never go hungry, and whoever believes in me will never be thirsty.'"

John 6:35, NIV)

If you guessed that this chapter was about food, then you'd be right. Well, mostly. The fact is, foster children are hungry for so many things, food is truly only a small portion of their needs in the totality of everything they're missing. However, it is a challenging one.

Before jumping into food issues, let me list a number of other obvious (and maybe not so obvious) things kids in the foster care system are literally starving for and/or craving: love, attention, affection, nurturing, cuddles/hugs, joy, laughter, forgiveness, trust (both giving and getting), safety, security, stability, freedom, education, everyday learning, sleep, healthy nutrition, exercise, time, hope, grace, mercy, faith, to belong, to succeed, to see their family, to grieve,… a chance for a future. Did any of these surprise you? If so which one(s)? You might want to discuss it with your spouse and social worker. This list is not exhaustive, but it hits on the big desires nearly all foster kids have.

When we met our three kids, ages five, five, and three, they were really into food: junk food that is. Specifically, McDonald's. The second day we spent with them we took them to their favorite place, McDonald's, and they proceeded to tell us exactly what they wanted: Happy Meals, which included chicken nuggets, fries, soda, and, of course, a toy. We said "no" to the soda and opted for apple juice and milk instead. My daughter wanted chocolate milk, but we said "no" to that as well. I could tell immediately she was going to be a picky eater.

We took them to a movie that day, after McDonald's, which none of them, except my daughter, could sit through. We saw their high energy levels and ADHD tendencies right away. After the movie we decided to stop by a grocery store so we could pick out some fruit and enjoy that when we got them home. We took them through the fruit aisles and watched with great surprise that they knew what very few fruits actually were. They could name apple, banana, and strawberries, and my daughter identified a watermelon, but that was it!

We grabbed strawberries, pineapple, watermelon, plums, and tangerines. We also showed them what a kiwi, papaya, and dragon fruit looked like. They "oohed" and "ahhed" as we picked them up one at a time, told them the name, and asked them to hold them. Why not teach them while experiencing new things together? We purchased our fruit and went home for a fun afternoon. We thought it would be exciting to watch their faces light up as they tasted new foods for the first time.

As expected, my daughter was not interested in anything she hadn't previously tasted (foreshadowing here on so many things she would "dig her heels in" down the road). She did have a piece of watermelon, but that was it. The boys were more daring. I saw a bit of hesitation in my eldest, but as soon as I took a bite and made all the "mmm" sounds, he wanted to give the fruits a try. Plums were not well received, but they liked the others. My youngest son proved to be quite the 'foodie" and had a discerning palate for his young age! To this day, he still tries just about everything and actually dislikes very little.

However, once the kids joined us in our home, the real test was eating regular healthy, balanced meals all the time and greatly reduced amounts of fast food. They all liked sweets, of course. Getting sugar out of their diet was a problem. Just like TV, they had been indulged with sweets, getting cookies and cake almost daily. It's not that they never got those things with us, but we were much more careful with their diets and how much sugar they ate.

Before we got our kids, we learned that our youngest son had a bowel obstruction as a toddler and had spent some time in the hospital. Luckily, surgery wasn't necessary, but he came to us with a very bloated abdomen and often complained of stomach pain. We were told by the pediatrician that a healthy diet would take awhile to counterbalance the poor diet he'd had for so long. We even found that he was lactose intolerant and quickly switched him to almond milk, which we all enjoy. It took a solid six months for his body to change from the bloated toddler to a healthy four-year-old. On the flip side, my daughter was skinny as could be and wouldn't gain an ounce. And, my eldest son was a wee bit chubby and gained weight very fast. They were all so different!

In foster parent training, we learned what to look out for in children with food issues. Some would hoard food because it may not have been readily available, or food was used in an abusive way by keeping it from them as a form of punishment. Tools on how to handle this were shared, and we were grateful that our kids didn't appear to have any of those issues. Or so we thought…

It didn't happen as foster kids, but later after we adopted our kids we noticed the two older ones acting more sneaky than usual one summer. It turned out they were hoarding snacks and secretly eating them together while hiding the evidence. This all arose when I was on a health journey to lose weight and had rid the house of all junk. They, apparently, were on a quest to make sure the sweetest stuff in the house didn't get tossed! My son also admitted he was always hungry. We explained as he grew up, he would get more hungry as his body changed, but he needed to talk to us so we could determine just how much more he required for his size.

We thought that would be the end of it, but just a few months ago, we caught my daughter sneaking my diet infusers (berry flavored mixes to add to water so I can get more water in throughout the day). These have caffeine in them, plus they're for adults—not kids—and she did not have my permission to take them. This one bothered me because the infusers are generally quite expensive, and I need them for my continued health journey. My daughter has always been sneaky and taken things that didn't belong to her. I've caught her sneaking candy, gum, and other sweet things. She has even stolen sweet things from other kids' lunches (this is another topic for discussion, but since it's food related I thought I'd mention it).

So, we have definitely had our share of food issues. But overall, it has been fairly easy compared to other foster kids with serious food issues. The best thing I ever did was lose over a hundred pounds; my husband lost over forty by eating healthy and modeling it for our kids. We also taught them how to read labels. We all needed to reduce our sugar intake and eat less processed foods. We gave up spaghetti and replaced it with zucchini noodles called "zoodles." We began removing buns from burgers and reduced a lot of unnecessary white flour and other simple carbs replacing them with complex carbs, fiber, five fruits and vegetables a day, lean protein, and low sodium. We all share a heart-healthy diet, and it shows in my kids as well as myself and husband. God's whole foods are always better than man's over-processed ones and it's our job to teach our kids the healthy way to eat for life!

Reflection

We know our children come to us starving for various needs no child should ever go without. Love, trust, and stability are at the top of that emotional list, but there are other essential elements missing as well. It's important to remember in the midst of physical needs, such as food and water, that we can feed them healthy foods to consume while modeling healthy behaviors to match. But the spiritual nourishment they need is just as important. It starts with helping them recognize they can always count on the Lord to provide for them so they are never in want for anything ever again.

Prayer

Heavenly Father, help me to teach my children how to live a healthy life in every aspect, not just to eat healthy foods and maintain a healthy lifestyle, but to create a habit of looking to You for all their needs first. Help me to instruct them in Your ways so they will always hunger and thirst after righteousness. Give me grace and patience as I break through strongholds relating to food in their life so they will grow strong and healthy in body, mind, and spirit. I humbly ask this in Your Son's precious name, Jesus. Amen!

Simply Dedicated

25. Simply Insane

By Kim S. Bushey, A Fellow Handmaiden

" Those who sow with tears will reap with songs of joy. Those who go out weeping carrying seed to sow, will return with songs of joy, carrying sheaves with them." (Psalm 126:5-6, NIV)

December 1, 2019, was a happy, calm day… well at least for me, in this home of eight children. A Sunday, no appointments!... and then ramp it up here comes Monday, the 2nd, and off we went, to what would be a couple of months of insanity. Ready, set, hold on!

My daughter Self-control needed Vitamin D3, and her cholesterol was high. We might need to consider medication, the doctor said. We were also concerned about her thyroid and would need to recheck in three months.

I got back home for the next appointment with Goodness, for her therapy group to review. Sounded easy enough, but let's not forget I teach the children all at home, and some need constant reminders of personal hygiene and what to eat or not to eat, and I don't know about you, but I don't have a maid or a cook.

Now came the 3rdof December, and I was up early so I could decorate for the holidays. The appliance repairman was coming because the dryer has been broken and we've been hanging laundry for ten people in the basement on racks—that was fun! He has great news: The parts needed to be ordered; the motor was shot, Ugh! Then I sent some older kids to the store while I kept decorating. I got off the ladder and wondered where I left the hammer as I began to move the ladder.

SLAM! Searing pain gripped me. I was dizzy holding the ladder, still slammed against the stairway, and it took me a few moments to realize the hammer was on top of the ladder.

Pain, lots of pain. Am I bleeding? Can I push the ladder off me? Can I walk, or am I going to fall down?

I made it downstairs to tell the kids what happened in case they needed to call for help. The baby was sleeping, and I thanked the Lord for that. I got an ice pack for my throbbing head and tried to think.

When the older kids got home, I decided I really should get checked out because the pain is so bad. I was thinking I could drive, and my daughter Love said NO WAY! She said she would take me to the hospital and come back to care for the children at home. Good idea!

I had a CT because they thought I may very well have had a brain bleed, and I can thank the Lord again, I didn't have a brain bleed. My husband came straight to the hospital from work and brought me home. It was very difficult for the next month or so to think clearly and out of the question to multitask for weeks. Now that IS a handicap! Keep that in mind as you keep reading.

I'd promised my children a year before that they could have a craft fair at our home this year and it was planned and happening in just a few short days. All the invitations were already sent, all the crafts were all made, so my mom and papa came to help. I was so sick, trying to talk to people, trying to focus on what they are saying, trying to smile, and this is simply awful.

Monday rolled around and it's back to therapy for kiddos, teaching, GI appointment, and the stove breaks! Are you kidding? First the dryer, now the stove!

My head hurts and I had to drive an hour away to take Self-control to her appointment with the neurologist, who said because of the terminal diagnosis her biological brother, Gentleness, was given last November, all siblings should have MRIs because of issues we are having. He also said we really needed to see neuropsychologist for Self-control.

We were scheduled to do a radio interview for Make-A-Wish tomorrow, and I was feeling very emotional. Laundry was piling up. It was hard to think. I still felt sick. I got through the interviews but my head felt as if it was going to explode.

Later on, I stopped by the adoption agency to show them how big the kids were getting and fellowship for a while. I found out my friend, who is another adoptive mama, was pregnant. It was the best news I've had in a while, and I was SO happy!

All within a couple weeks it was my husband's birthday, MRI for one of the three that needed them, then the next two MRIs were scheduled somewhere else on another day, everything was at least an hour away. We had to wait for the results for this one. PUSH on.

Then it was Self-control's birthday and the next day Love's birthday. Ok, so I'm not a boring birthday kind of mom, some of my kids never had a cake, let alone a party, before we had them, so we tried to make it a big deal.

Kids had a piano and violin recital and the baby has been sick. I've had her to the doctor twice in the past week because she wasn't breathing well. Her throat was swollen, she was not sleeping, and neither was I. I was supposed to be resting so the concussion could get better. I had to miss the recital, it was the first one I've ever missed, and I was sad, and tired, and stressed.

I tried to get ready for the birthday party while the baby slept, but I couldn't put the monitor down because she wasn't breathing well, and then it happened. She stopped, no breath, no wheezing, no sound. My heart leaps into my throat, and I run.

Upon my abruptly scooping her up, she let out a gasping scream, and we both cried. Everyone came home for the party and the repairman came to fix the clothes washer. Yes, I did say "washer," because that broke too!!!!! Dryer, stove, now washer, ugh!

I cancelled the advanced tickets for the movie for dad and the teens, signed the paper for the repairman, left the guests, and took off to go to the nearest hospital with the baby. We were transported by ambulance to the larger children's hospital where we waited in the small, hot ER room while it's debated whether she goes to ICU or the floor. At about 2 a.m., we were finally admitted to the floor with my precious little one where we stayed for a couple days until she was well enough to come home.

It was soon Christmas—um, yes, if you missed it, I'm still in December! I make the cake, baked bread, picked up the milk, got to celebrate, and pretty soon I was very dizzy. That's odd, I still have bad headaches, but I have not been dizzy. Hmm, is there a cat here? Yes, and that's why I can hardly stand, and my heart is pounding hard—I'm allergic to cats. I have to go home NOW!

Days later, two more MRI's were completed, and we waited again for results. Baby Goodness was done with the antibiotics and started a little fever again. I was fervently praying about everything. She has been losing weight, and I was very concerned, so I called the gastrointestinal department again.

We changed her tube feedings, hoping that would help. We did therapy for her, and talked to the neurologist again about results for Self-control. I could NEVER do all of this without JESUS!

It's January, New Year's Day—it will be better! What's this? A very disturbing text from that friend who is pregnant. She was losing the baby, and then it happened. My sadness turned to anger. I have been through many things and have gotten through all of them without this anger, but now, for someone else, I was angry. Why?

Her heart was grieving and I always try to be supportive. I usually don't want to be angry, but I just couldn't understand. I was finally able to give in to God being God and remembered that I am not, and He is always good, and I told Him I was sorry. He never wanted death,

He wants life and that more abundantly for us...hold on, PUSH through.

Now it was Patience's birthday and the food pantry gave us a beautiful cake. I didn't need to make one, I just decorated the one we got. I had to teach, attend therapy, work on getting baby Goodness a wheelchair, signed up for some help with bills since my husband has needed to be home to help. He was starting a new business and was working outside the home.

Then it was time to take two kids to the orthodontist. I sensed God was telling me to start a speaking business and start writing those devotionals. He's been telling me to do for years...WHAT?! Right NOW?! Umm, excuse me Lord, have You noticed my life lately??

Next, Kindness needed an EEG. He had to wear the EEG machine at home for a couple of days with a cute white turban and lots of wires. Now we needed to send that back and wait for results. We had lots of appointments that week, therapy, orthodontist again, neurology, piano, violin, a long-term support person came in this week so we can get some additional help with the children's needs. Dishes, laundry, cooking, cleaning, it never stops… I just want to curl up in my sweet husband's arms and cry, and he lets me and comforts me so I can PUSH on.

Then we got the results for the other two MRIs. Joy has a spot on her brain that will have to be monitored with a follow-up MRI in six months, so for now we just wait… This waiting thing is growing me, and I think I have some growing pains.

Kindness might need neurosurgery, we will have to go to the surgeon for consultation. Make more appointments. I took all seven older kids to the dentist, made more appointments for the dentist for fillings, took baby Goodness to the cardiologist and GI doctor.

Then the weekend was over, back to appointments, another class for me to learn more about how to help Self-control, so she doesn't lie so much…hopefully. I had the baby checked out again because she still didn't want to eat, and I was wondering if her throat was okay or not. I packed an overnight bag as I thought I may end up staying at the hospital with her overnight. I also had to see the neurosurgeon with Kindness—he needed more MRIs.

While we are at the doctor's office, my husband gets a much-needed text from his former boss saying he would like to have him back to work and that he is more than willing to work around our kiddos' appointments. That was a miracle in the union construction field! After the appointments were done, it's all got arranged, he went back to work that following Monday! That was a HUGE relief because now the second mortgage is used up and credit cards are maxed.

I got to come home with everyone because baby Goodness was doing better than I thought. We made it home before the big snowstorm hit, so Praise the LORD! We started a fire in the fireplace, all was calm. I was at the table so thankful, thinking of all that God had just done. Things were pretty quiet, so I took out the garden plan and my seeds and started making a list of when I should begin with planting, and I wanted love to end this insanity with a sweet ending, but… all the sudden I hear a piercing scream from my husband, who was in the garage working on making shelves. The first thing that came to my mind was a shelf falling and hitting his head because of the hammer incident on my own head. BUT before I can even got out the door I heard him screaming again and again.

I'm terrified as I open the door and hear him scream that he cut off his finger. He was bleeding everywhere through the gloves. I didn't see his thumb, only a limp glove. I was panicking and trying to pray. The kids were crying. I grabbed keys, tried to gather the children; it was a nightmare! Except it was real.

I drove to the nearest hospital, in a terrible snowstorm, worried about the blood spurting out of my husband, trying to call for help for the kids, trying to calm him…crying to Jesus for help!!!!!!! In the hospital the glove, shirt, and sweatshirt are cut off to find out it was not just the thumb: this part of his hand is "ground" off by the angle grinder with the 4 ½-inch chainsaw blade on it, all the way across the palm of his hand. His thumb is hanging on by a small amount of tissue. I try to calm him, to no avail.

He was bleeding for a very long time as we wait for a flight for life ambulance in the storm. It took many more hours until we were in the next hospital and got him prepped for emergency surgery. He was still bleeding, and the surgeon said if it was any other finger we would just remove it. He said he would try his best to save the thumb, but he couldn't make any promises. By then I was in a huge waiting room, all alone. It was eerie with silence, the snowstorm was raging outside. My children were with friends, and I waited. I got down on my knees and prayed. I laid down on one of the many couches and cried.

Finally, the surgeon came to me and said he was able to reattach his thumb and sew up his hand. He said it is very severe because it wasn't cut across but ground off, and his bone looked like sawdust. He had to pull tendons, nerves, and muscle from the upper forearm to attach. My husband might need another surgery later on. It will be months of therapy and recovery. He wasn't sure if he would be a framing carpenter again, ever. PUSH, January isn't over!

My husband stayed in ICU after the procedure and woke up screaming in pain. This lasted the whole night, into the next morning, and it was nerve-racking. My husband has had open heart surgery and has been in terrible pain, but he never screamed like this. He hardly ever complains at all. When things finally got under control and we were able to come home, I was so thankful because I knew it could have been worse....

Our oldest daughter Faithfulness and new boyfriend came to town for a four-day visit. My mom and papa were be there too. Faithfulness lives in another state now so wants her friend and her family to come and stay too, although they don't end up coming because her mom is put on hospice.

The new week began, and life didn't stop. Teaching, appointments, Kindness' birthday, therapy for multiple children and now my husband as well, paperwork, dentist, eye doctor, got the windshield fixed, lessons, prescriptions, grocery shop, cardiology, GI, x-rays, hearing aids fixed, fillings, OMG, Self-control forgot to put the tray on the highchair, and baby Goodness fell out!!!!! Another trip to the ER since she's on blood thinners and I'm was so scared!... Yes, this last sentence was all in one week!

I thank God again after a long wait and a CT to find out there was no brain bleed, just a big bonk on her little head.

Simply Dedicated

Please, Lord, can February be better…it's the day before my birthday, kids are sick, and Kindness would have a complex neurosurgery in ten days, and I'm writing this for the Love of Jesus, my husband, my children, and for you. PUSH on!

"A woman giving birth to a child has pain because her time has come; but when her baby is born she forgets the anguish because of her joy that a child is born into the world."

(John 16:21, NIV)

I pondered this verse one miserable morning. I was so tired I needed Jesus to tell me I could go on—I could keep pushing! As I thought and prayed about the verse I'd just read, the thought came to me of how good God is, and I wondered more about how He made provision for the "woman in labor."

Not having any children physically, I decided to look up what happens to a woman's body during labor and delivery. I knew some things because I've been privileged to witness the miracle of birth before, but I had never researched details. As I did, I found out the blood supply of the woman is increased 30 to 50 percent during pregnancy. The heart is being exercised continually more with the increase and gaining endurance by pumping this extra volume. Labor pushes the heart to further limits, and the PUSH abruptly changes the pressure and flow of the blood. While I sat there thinking about how great and faithful our God is to make all these provisions for the woman in labor and delivery far in advance, it occurred to me I've been equipped in advance as well. God has made every provision for me to push through "all these trials which are temporary and light afflictions in the face of an eternal glory" (2 Corinthians 4:17).

The LORD gives labor coaches, nurses, and a midwife or a doctor to help with the birth of a baby, and He gave us people who brought meals, dropped off a gift, gave us a hug, prayed with us, and came to care for our children. He gave us the Great Physician to help us deliver faith, hope, and love to those around us. For all these things we are thankful.

God bless you as you PUSH on!

Reflection

- In what ways is the Lord asking to PUSH?
- How is God providing what you need in order to push through the challenges that you and your family are facing?

Prayer

Oh Jesus, thank You for being the Great Physician. Thank You for loving me so deeply and helping when I'm weary. Thank You for interceding for me so I can become more like You. Help me when I lose focus on You. Show me how only You can work all these things for good because I love You and You have called me for Your purposes. Remind me I can carry this cross because with You I can do all things. I don't want to do it on my own, and I can't. Empower me now to encourage and strengthen others who are weary so they can keep pushing through to deliver faith, hope, and love. AMEN.

26. Simply Inspired

By Kirsten Marie Peterson

"... But those who hope in the Lord will renew their strength. They will soar on wings like eagles they will run and not grow weary. They will walk and not grow faint"
(Isaiah 40:31, NIV)

I always knew I would be a mom; I don't think there was any inspiration necessary for my goal to be a mom—it literally was who I was born to be. Quite honestly, it is the only calling I ever felt I had. I played with dolls as a child, always giving them names I felt my own children would have. I knew in my youth that I would have six children, two biological and four adopted. I started babysitting at eleven years old, and continued until I was sixteen and got a grocery store job that gobbled up my weekends. I dated every man with the nagging thought "Will he make a good daddy?" which, by the way, is NOT the way to start a long-term relationship! I started researching baby names right after college because I just knew I would fall in love with a wonderful man, get married, and start my family in my early twenties. Well, thirty rolled up on me, and I was not in a serious relationship and was starting to feel that biological clock ticking.

After a few pity parties to friends about not being married with kids yet, a friend had a rather inspirational idea—what about adoption? I considered domestic and international private adoption, but honestly, as a teacher I didn't have the thousands of dollars necessary for that route to a family. (At that time, I was unaware of the fundraising efforts many churches use to offset international adoption costs for families, or the possibility of bank loans for private domestic adoptions.) When my investigating adoption routed me to the topic of foster care, I was intrigued but was also very concerned that I wouldn't be able to handle the intense emotions of caring for a child with all of my heart and then having to say goodbye when the children were reunited with their biological family members. Soon after, I heard you could adopt foster children if the state decides to terminate parental rights for the child's long-term welfare. I was thrilled to discover this—this was the way to becoming a mom after my lifetime of yearning and dreaming. I figured I would adopt a little girl, find the man of my dreams, and continue on with building my family of six children. (I am a bit embarrassed that my yearning for a family is what brought me to the idea of adoption, and not the notion of helping a child find a forever home, but I feel the need to write from a place of authenticity.)

There was a lot of silence from the phone when I first became a licensed foster home. I was discouraged, frustrated, and confused. Where were all these foster children I heard about all the time? Eventually I went with a different agency and started getting calls. I turned down so many that I just felt I wasn't suited for due to the age or needs of the child. Then I got the call about a two-year-old little girl whose biological mom's rights were already terminated and her biological dad's rights were in the termination process. I went to meet Kaya, and within ten seconds of setting eyes on her, that megawatt smile caused my heart to flutter and I KNEW she and I were destined to be a family. After a couple of months to transition, Kaya came to permanently live with me. I knew we were an excellent mom and daughter fit from day one but yearned for that judge to finalize and confirm that Kaya was forever a permanent member of my family. At age three, her adoption was finalized, and I was an official MOM in the eyes of the law.

Fast forward and I now am an adoptive mom to four children, two teen girls, one teen boy, and one preteen boy. I also am a foster mom to a nearly two-year-old that adoption proceedings have been started on. Over the last seventeen years, I have found many things about being a mom, specifically a foster-to-adopt mom, that have inspired me. I never had any doubts that I would be well suited for the role of mom. I assumed growing up that I would be the type of mom to be fully involved in her children's lives and raise them in a traditional manner. I had an idea that I would raise my children to be lifelong learners, be respectful of others, challenge the status quo if they saw things were morally or ethically wrong, and grow to be adults who inspired other foster children. But I had absolutely no idea how greatly my children would inspire me to truly grow into the best version of myself on a daily basis!

The Merriam-Webster dictionary defines inspiration as "the action or power of moving the intellect or emotions" and "the act of influencing or suggesting opinions." Before becoming a mom, I assumed my actions and simply my parenting would be inspirational to my children, but how I was wrong! My children simply have inspired me from the moment I have met each one of them. It would be too difficult to list or name all the ways each child has inspired me to personal greatness in my role as mom, so I have chosen to group their influence in my life into three categories: influencing me as a foster home advocate, influencing me as a mental health advocate, and influencing me to be more cognizant of race and racial relations both in my immediate circle and on a larger institutional and societal level.

I knew dealing with the Department of Children and Family Services, (DCFS), as it is a multi-layered state bureaucracy, would be a challenge to my patience. I prefer common-sense approaches and also like to think outside the box when solving problems. In my experience, neither of these methods is utilized by DFCS. Add into that a group of good-hearted but overworked and underpaid caseworkers and licensing workers, and you have an absolute test to anyone's patience. Rather than let that drive me away, I decided to let this ongoing test of my patience inspire me to become an advocate for all foster children by changing the system when and where I could.

I have kept notes on what I thought might be ways to true and purposeful change. I kept notes from my friend's experiences in different states as well. Taking care of the most vulnerable children in society, those in foster care, who are already suffering the trauma of removal from their birth families, is a daunting task for any agency.

I see my children's faces and have renewed inspiration daily to help educate and empower families to challenge the inadequacies they see in their state's DCFS system whenever possible. I hope to become more active as a foster family trainer and an ongoing presence in state-wide meetings of foster parent and adoptive parent groups as my children grow more independent and my time frees up.

I have always been interested in anatomy and biology, but never did I realize how much being an adoptive mom to foster children would inspire me to delve into brain health, mental illness, and the ins and outs of birth trauma and familial/generational mental illness and trauma! I have learned oh so much over the past seventeen years about the umbrella that is mental health! Again this is an issue that is an ongoing inspiration, as I am always searching for a way to help my children who struggle with mental illness.

Finding appropriate psychiatrists, locating trauma informed counselors who actually take our insurance, and learning how to read up on the pros and cons of various suggested treatments has been a challenge at times. Even deciding how knowledgeable and involved my children should be in their own mental health care has been difficult. However, I am constantly inspired by my children's resilience, and that inspiration drives me to make the next phone call or search the next medical site for more information on their diagnosis and treatment options.

The other significant area where my children have unknowingly inspired me is probably the most obvious to people as they look at a family photo of my children and me. I am white, and I was raised in predominantly white areas in Wisconsin and Florida. Although I don't think I was raised with racist ideology, I certainly was raised with white privilege but didn't even consider that term or social issue until I became mom to a black child. I vowed before the judge at her adoption to do everything I could to make myself the minority in situations like my daughter's church and school so that she would be around children with her racial background predominantly. I thought it quite important that my daughter, and then of course my subsequent children, feel confident and comfortable among all races, and I certainly couldn't do that if I continued to attend my same white-dominated church, grocery store, neighborhood, etc. Prior to being a foster mom, a typical week's schedule of places and people was filled with wonderful, kind, generous, and intelligent people—but they all happened to be white. I felt inspired to change that for the sake of my children. As a result, MY life has been greatly enriched in ways I never thought possible. I have enjoyed diversifying the places we go to as a family, the church and school experiences we have had, and expanding my own circle of friends to encompass all races, many nationalities, and socioeconomic/faith backgrounds. This diversification of my own life was a direct result of my children inspiring me to push beyond my own comfort limits into something new. For that I am forever grateful!

Becoming a foster and adoptive parent has enriched my life in ways I never could have imagined. I do not think I would have made even a fraction of the changes in my life without my darlings as my inspiration!

Reflection

"Mom, mom, mom, MOM!"

Familiar?

In order to continue being inspired by my children, I need to be in a zone where I am alert enough and patient enough to hear their hearts as they tell me a simple story from their school day or take my time to watch or join them as they play. With an ever increasing demand on a busy involved parent's time, slowing down and observing, listening to your children, is of utmost importance. But how?

Starting the day with a miracle morning approach can work wonders to set the stage for a successful and intentional day. Setting aside a half hour or hour before anyone awakens allows for a time of gratitude, prayer, personal development, exercise, and review of the list for the day, including blocked out time for listening to your child/children in an unhurried way. This time of solitude can make all the difference. By starting our day asking for God's guidance on being an intentional parent, not just in listening to our children, but also blocking out time to act on what they inspire us to do, is critical to being a continually inspired parent!

Prayer

Most Holy Father, thank You for allowing me to continue on my earthly journey. I know You understand the goodness in my heart and my desire to truly help others. Please fill me with inspirational ideas to better the lives of my children, as well as the lives of the broader foster child community. Please give me the ongoing positive energy necessary to implement true and lasting change. Thank You for always guiding my faithful footsteps. In Your Holy Name I pray.   Amen.

27. Simply Joyful, even when everyone is puking around you!

By Kim S. Bushey, A Fellow Handmaiden

"Be joyful in hope, patient in affliction, faithful in prayer." (Romans 12:12, NIV)

It was cold outside, and we were all inside, puke buckets on top of puke buckets, and accident poopy bottoms! Makeshift beds on the couches, cots in the living room, and pure exhaustion! All eight kids were sick. My husband and I were so tired, we just wanted a little sleep, I wanted out of this mess! LORD, help them, help ME! Then I heard a still, small voice, "In ALL things give thanks." UGH! NOW!? Like right NOW? How? Then a memory came flooding into my mind and heart.

Years ago, I just had three children and was taking care of my husband's grandmother. I was knee deep in snot and poopy diapers. We were living in the basement of Chad's grandparents; Grandpa had passed away, and Grandma needed help, so we left our wonderful farm of five years to care for her. I was teaching my eight-year-old daughter at home. OK so if you got a picture of a lovely finished area, forget it–I mean some of it was, but not all of it, and ALL of it had not been used in many years… well except by mice and spiders!

Lots of cleaning later, I was standing one day in front of a changing table cleaning another poopy bottom, and I asked

God, "What am I doing here? All I do is wipe butts and noses. GOD, I thought I was going to do something for You, something that matters! I thought I would change the world?! All I do is wipe butts and noses!" (I said it twice in case He didn't hear me the first time.) Some tears of self-pity ran down my face as I got no reply.

Not long after that, Grandma was put on hospice. We kept her at home, but the thought was tough to swallow. Not only would we lose this woman we loved, but now thoughts of where we would live began to creep into my mind. That same week, our precious son was returned to his biological mother, gone without a thing I could do about it. She'd been caught committing fraud and "needed" him back.

My heart was breaking. We went to church that Sunday and came home to our daughter's precious pony lying down in a strange position in the pasture. She'd fallen and broken her hip; we all knew we'd have to put her down, and my husband, myself, and our daughter stood in the pasture and cried. We cried for Grandma, we cried for our son, we cried for the pony and for ourselves. It was one of the most difficult weeks of my life.

That is depressing, so I won't leave you there. Come with me ten months later to a very large and lovely home we were renting. Our son came home! He was vastly different. He'd lost all his roly-poly chubbiness, he lost his smile, he lost trust, he even forgot how to chew and swallow food! But he was home! As I stood in front of the changing table one day changing his poopy bottom looking at his skin and bones and those shallow eyes of suspicion pondering all he may have been through, I clearly heard the LORD speak into my soul:

"Now, do you see? What you do matters."

So many tears had run down my cheeks that day, and today in the midst of diarrhea and puke it was all I needed to "encourage myself in the LORD" and carry on, thanking God for my children and finding joy even in the midst of this mess all around me!

Reflection

Isn't it hard to rejoice always? I fail! It's so much easier though when I think to ask God for help. If I don't I get tempted to whine and complain. Jesus is always ready to come to my aide. He may not take the trial away, at least the way I think it should happen but, he WILL use it for good because we Love Him and He called us! Let us be truly thankful for the family He's given us even when there's a mess all around. We are doing what is important to the LORD. What we do matters, it changes lives, we share His love and grace with others even in all the little things. I want to encourage you, you matter! What you do matters! You are treasured and dearly loved. Thank you for all you do even when no one sees the love you are pouring out. May you be filled to overflowing with the joy of the LORD and may your spirit spring up like a well! I'm sending you blessings from my noisy house, the older kids are playing cards with daddy, the radio is playing, the little boys are playing with cars loudly, the baby is smiling and playing and they are all discussing what I'm making for supper... lol JOY!

> "Bless the LORD oh my soul and forget not all His benefits"
> Psalm 103:2 NIV

How can you rejoice in Lord in this season in your life?

What benefits has God blessed you with during this season?

Prayer

Lord Jesus, I want to recall Your goodness to me especially when I need it most! Please remind me to recount all Your kindnesses to me. Don't let Satan have a foothold in my heart. I am sorry for whining and complaining, please forgive me. I am so thankful Your mercies are new every morning! I want to steward all you put in my hands well so help me LORD. I need You. Amen.

Simply Dedicated

28. Simply Labeled Wrong

By Julie P. Watson

"I have told you these things, so that in me you may have peace. In this world you will have trouble. But take heart! I have overcome the world."
(John 16:33, NIV)

Whether you're a new foster parent or you've done this for awhile, one thing you won't be short on are acronyms. There seems to be acronyms for everything from injury reports, to the monthly clothes count, to court documents, etc. But, some of the most important acronyms are the ones kids get labeled with from psychiatrists, therapists, specialists, doctors, and teachers. Sometimes these become labels for life, but they shouldn't!

When we first got our placement, our eldest son had just been diagnosed, only three weeks prior, with Attention Deficit Hyperactive Disorder (ADHD). He had also been diagnosed with Oppositional Defiance Disorder (ODD). We learned about these diagnoses in our foster training six months beforehand, but I had to inquire again what exactly ODD meant for this precious five-year-old.

WebMD.com defines it as follows:

ODD is a condition in which a child displays an ongoing pattern of an angry or irritable mood, defiant or argumentative behavior, and vindictiveness toward people in authority. The child's behavior often disrupts the child's normal daily activities, including activities within the family and at school.

It might be expected then that ODD is commonly diagnosed in foster children, as our Foster Family Agency (FFA) explained to us during the case review before placement. Within the first two hours of meeting our children, we easily identified that as accurate in our oldest son. That boy sometimes had a look in his eyes that said he was gonna rip your head off if you even looked at him funny. Thankfully, we saw so many other wonderful qualities, we didn't let that scare us. But, oh the behaviors foster care brings into your home! Whoa!! God help us when our son was mad at us—we have a lot of "scars" in our home where he made his anger quite known (i.e., peeling paint off the walls; breaking things intentionally; carving things into the walls, windows, and dining room table; etc).

Vindictiveness is extremely difficult to handle when you have multiple children, especially two with ADHD and ODD. You see, my daughter was diagnosed about a year later at the request of her kindergarten teacher. However, her ODD displayed itself in manipulative vindictiveness, passive-aggressive anger, and defiance. My son has always been easier to figure out because he wears his emotions on his sleeve. My daughter is stubborn and controlling. She has put up a mighty large wall that has taken us years to crack through. She keeps her emotions locked up—much more than her brothers. So when she takes her anger out on someone, it's usually something we have to become detectives to figure out, since she's also a compulsive liar (unfortunately, lying is quite common, and very difficult to stop when they have made it a habit for so long).

Thankfully, our youngest son skipped all the labels. He had some speech and development delays, but his big issue was being socially withdrawn. He used to hide behind furniture when the other two were chasing each other in anger. If he was frustrated, scared, or unsure, he simply withdrew and hid. We worked through that with a special therapist and doing play therapy, but I was thankful to have him home with me alone for the first year (other than half days at preschool three days a week). We got a lot of quality "Mommy and me time" in.

Since he was only three and a half and didn't speak much when we got him (he would point and grunt when he wanted something), it gave me an opportunity to work with him alone while the other two attended kindergarten. Those were some of my favorite times during that highly stressful first year. We sang songs; did verbal exercises so he could say his letters correctly; played games; did tons of puzzles; built with Legos; learned colors, numbers, and opposites; and cuddled and tickled a lot. I rocked him to sleep before every nap. Essentially, I loved him up as much as I could to replace what was never received. This precious boy of mine went into foster care at sixteen months old, so I had a lot of "filling up the love cup" to do. When children don't receive this kind of attention, love, and play early on, they don't develop social, life, or coping skills. He didn't have any coping skills in dealing with the craziness of his siblings' behaviors, but he learned with my help.

Besides ADHD, which my kids have two different forms of (there are at least seven different forms of ADHD), I also had all three tested for Fetal Alcohol Syndrome (FAS). Since my kids were each exposed to alcohol in utero, and my eldest especially showed signs of delays in specific areas, it was important to have testing done. The outcome was rather frustrating, however. My oldest son had five out of six markers for FAS. The doctor literally said, "It means he probably has it, but because he only has five out of six markers for it, I can't officially diagnose him as having FAS." Well, where do you go with that?

A person with FAS has permanent brain damage. The part of the brain that gets damaged depends on what developmental stage the fetus is in when exposed to alcohol. Obviously, if the unborn child is exposed for the duration of the gestation period, there are multiple areas likely affected. Within my son, the executive functioning (frontal lobe) part of the brain is damaged. That's the cause-and-effect portion of the brain. You know, the one that tells you if you cross the street without looking you might get hit, so don't try it. My son had to learn everything many times over to finally "get it."

You see, permanent brain damage can never be cured or healed; you can only create new neural pathways to learn what's naturally missing. Do that enough times with enough issues and he will eventually be able to apply that learned logic/knowledge to new situations... hopefully. Sadly, most FAS children are developmentally/behaviorally half their chronological age. So, a ten-year-old would developmentally be about five. Our son is a bit higher than that. He would be about a seven-year-old in that scenario. But, we see daily challenges for him in making healthy and safe decisions. We will continue to love and help him learn until he's ready to make it on his own in this world, but it may be harder for him than his siblings (both showed fewer FAS markers).

There are many other labels out there which you will likely learn about in your foster parent training. Rest assured—LABELS DO NOT DEFINE THE CHILD. Our children are all quite intelligent and going places! We always tell them, "You may have ADHD, ODD, or FAS, but it does not have you!" We have taught them, through therapy and our own research, how to manage their conditions and behaviors (e.g., belly breathing to stop "flipping their lid" and other calming techniques). We have done specialized therapy, including Occupational Therapy (OT) which notably had the most positive effect. We found essential oils that helped calm them as well as assist with focus and clarity. Medicine was needed, however, as their ADHD is extreme and it was affecting their learning in school. (A child who loses confidence in school quickly spirals downward and is delayed even further).

Most importantly, we remind the kids still that God uniquely and masterfully designed them! While He didn't "give" them their conditions, He allowed them to endure so they could OVERCOME with His help. By overcoming our life's difficulties we can then testify to God's goodness, mercy, and faithfulness now and always.

Reflection

God continues to mold and make us into His image. No matter what labels your children come with or are given, they need to be reminded of how God defines them—for that's what truly matters! They are loved and precious in His sight. He delights in them, sings over them, prays for them, and rejoices with them. He cares about all their concerns, but He especially wants them to understand that they were created in His image. They were, in fact, fearfully and wonderfully created to overcome the things in this world so they could forever live with Christ in the next.

Prayer

Dear Jesus, You know better than anyone else how precious these children are—for You created each one as a masterpiece by Your hand and in Your image. Please guide me in every aspect of their care, especially with any medical or psychological labels placed upon them. Show me what's best for them and their specific needs so they will do all You've meant for them to accomplish in this life. Help me to instill in them that they were designed, with Your help, to overcome the difficult things in this world so that You can be glorified! I ask this in Your holy name, Lord. Amen!

Simply Dedicated

29 Simply Looks Different

By Brenda Wagenknecht

"Fathers, do not exasperate your children; instead, bring them up in the training and instruction of the Lord."
(Ephesians 6:4, NIV)

Over years of parenting, we have often heard many fellow parents comment to us, "That is not how I would have handled that situation!" Yes. We know. And honestly, we would have handled it differently also—up until the point we became parents to our adopted children and spent years researching how the brain responds to early trauma.

We both grew up in 1970s traditional American homes. You know, the parenting style of "do as you are told, don't talk about certain things, things are pretty black and white." We started down our parenting path with a basic idea of how we would parent: correct the wrongdoing and praise the appropriate behavior. It seemed so simple: boundaries and consequences. Until we actually had to apply it!

The first years of parenting were pretty typical. We comforted the cries, kissed the boo-boos, said "no" when a child got close to something hot, and spent any available time taking our children to see and experience new things in this world. A slight shift from traditional parenting began as we talked to our children about the difficult topics of adoption: talking about birth parents, teaching them about their heritage, and answering the tough questions like, "Where is my tummy mommy (birth mother)?" We were feeling pretty confident after doing quite a bit of research on the needs of our children.

Therapeutic Parenting by Sarah Naish and The Connected Child by Dr. Karyn Purvis helped transform our parenting style. We learned the basic understanding of how our childrens' brains were wired from trauma. Intense or prolonged stress rewires the brain and short-circuits the part of the brain that does critical thinking. Reactions happen without much thought when the amygdala becomes the processor of incoming stress. It responds in survival mode (fight/flight response). The brain that has lost the bond of their first attachment (in utero) to the biological mother, questions the attachment to any other. The road to developing trust with someone who lost their first attachment bond is long and hard.

We started to parent differently. We tried to find the sweet spot of balancing structure and nurture. Even through elementary years, our basic parenting strategies were not too obviously different. Things that looked different in our parenting were hard to notice for most observers: extra conversation when something stressful happened, giving choices (or "making a deal" as our youngest called it), and saying Yes more often than not to build trust. We were at times accused of not being hard enough on our children or "disciplining" severely enough. We would gently respond with explanations about using correction, guidance, and modeling as appropriately timed tools to point our children to the Savior through love, not through law.

There was, however, always a prevalence of unusual issues. All of our children, even our biological son, struggled with sensory processing issues. That meant we all struggled with the frustration of clothes that didn't feel right. The constant motion that one child required was so annoying to others. Mom wondered how to help our germaphobe child adjust next to the sibling's "touch and smell everything in sight" impulse. We adjusted our schedules (not to mention furniture) because of an intense need for things to be just in the right order. We all shared the heartache when tears flowed because the snuggly was not in bed. Dad tried to balance the need of loud rough-housing with physical safety concerns, and sometimes the scale tipped a little too far so bumps or bruises resulted.

Understanding the "why" behind these issues was a milestone step to learning how to help our child through them, without necessarily "correcting" traits that weren't wrong, even if they were annoying. Deep study in the development and function of the neurological systems unfolded an incredible opportunity to wonder at the God-created complexities of the brain! While only God can fully understand the incredible brain, studying neurodevelopment grew our understanding of the complex myriad of influences on human brain growth. Our children had very different backgrounds and experiences: stressful pregnancies, abuse and neglect, nutritional deficiencies, drug and alcohol exposure, separation from their biological mother at different ages, multiple moves, multiple cultural living situations, people in and out of their lives. . . .

Brenda's master's work in special education, followed by certification in an approach called HANDLE (Holistic Approach to Neurodevelopment and Learning Efficiency) changed our parenting even more. We learned to focus more on the "why" regarding our children's behavior as we constantly analysed their needs—all of their brain needs: physical, emotional, and spiritual. Our parenting began to look quite different. We continued to homeschool, which allowed us to provide them with their much-needed sensory regulation through physical movement. Daily routines included doing brain connecting activities, eating healthy fats to feed the brain, limited activities like screen time, and a lot of time for talking, thinking, and reflecting. We often heard, "So-and-so's parents do not make them do this!"

Then things started getting more complicated—peers became more important than Mom and Dad; American culture influenced our kids through T.V., movies, and the beginning of social media; and the hurts of this world that cannot be avoided stung. But most of all, as our children's brains developed, they started to question who they were and why God put them in a crazy family! The trauma our children had faced began to show more in the lack of trust, acting out, testing the boundaries. Our children asked more questions, often became more secretive, and needed more positive role models in their lives.

We continued to learn, mostly from our children. While our firm commitment to the truths found in the Bible did not change, we did ditch any "typical" parenting specifics if they lacked a basis in neuroscience. Some examples include: arbitrary punishments like grounding, authoritative power struggles, and even yelling. (That last one is really hard when Dad is tired or Mom has had it up to here....) We gave more choices and allowed our children to share in decision-making to teach them critical thinking. We put them in charge of some finances—making their own purchases and budgeting. We allowed them to try things like dying their hair. We had boundaries, and they were clear. When boundaries were crossed, natural consequences happened.

Things looked different in our parenting and in our family, but different was good. Our children did make mistakes and poor decisions, but they learned to trust us and to live independently. In fact, they are still growing, making mistakes, and learning. So are we as parents.

Do not exasperate, to say it another way, do not be so hard on children that they fail to trust, become fearful, or turn away. The core goal of discipline is teaching. It is not just consequences or punishment. Bring them up in the training and instruction of the Lord. Consequences must be explained every time, and followed by parental forgiveness. Take your child by the hand at their eye level, and calmly show them your sacrificial love. Parent with the Gospel. Discipline is showing, modeling, and molding the path; shaping behavior.

Reflection

- How can you build trust with my child?
- How can you say "Yes" or give choices?

Prayer

Dear Lord, You know the heart of my child. You know the hurt, the lack of trust, the questions of worth, and even the feelings of abandonment. Please give us strength as parents to have patience, love, and understanding to help heal their broken hearts and build connections of trust. In all we do, help us always point our children to You who have adopted us as Your own, given Your life for us, and continually guide us to trust You completely. Give us the words to say and the wisdom to parent according to our child's need, not social expectations. Forgive us when we mess up in our parenting. In Jesus' name. Amen.

30. Simply Loved

By Tracy Loken Weber

"Whatever you do... do it in love".
(1 Corinthians 16:14, NIV)

All we need is love. Deep down we all long for acceptance, friendship, to be liked and loved. To be included, called on, cared for. But, what do you do when love isn't enough? When the love you have for someone, something is overpowered by another vice? So many individuals struggle with their afflictions, struggle minute by minute to make the best decisions possible only in the end to lose all they held dear. Yet, in the end, letting go of a child is one of the most selfless acts of love one human being could ever do.

Our role as the primary caregiver is to love the child or children being entrusted to us unconditionally. To love them through their horrible past, to love them through the nightmares, to love them through the trauma of neglect, flashbacks. Even though we cannot see the past through their eyes, their tears, cries for help, and acting out behaviors are all battle calls for us to love on them even more. Lean down, lean in. Get to their level and try to understand what happened to them. Ask the question, "What happened to you?" Hold them close; tell them that they are safe, that they are loved, and that it's your job to keep them safe. That you will not allow anyone to hurt them. They are loved, and they are safe.

Sing the lullabies they never heard, read that extra book at bedtime, give them hugs and kisses, for all they really want is to be and feel loved. In the end, love, unconditional love, is all we need.

Reflection

- How can you show my love more?
- How can you be more patient? Show more grace to this child(ren)?
- What do you need to do to be more present in their everyday life?

Prayer

Heavenly Father, show me the way. Be the light during the dark times. Help me be patient, loving, and understanding. Guide my thoughts, words, and actions during times of tribulation. Shower me with grace, love, and understanding, so I may be at my very best during these times. Give me the patience so see my child through their manic episodes, understand where they are coming from, and allow healing to occur. In Your Son's name I pray, Amen.

31. Simply Messes, Memories and Mermaids

By Tracy Loken Weber

"But blessed is the one who trusts in the Lord, whose confidence is in him." (Jeremiah 17:7, NIV)

Messes. We all have them. Laundry, crumbs, dishes, let's face it, the list could go on and on. Before we expanded our home to include our furry child, Charlie, and followed by a sibling group of three, our home was untouched and clean. Yes, maybe a little mail clutter on the island, dishes in the sink, but the pillows on the sofa were still in place. Blankets folded and neatly lying laying on the back of the chair. We knew God was calling us to do more, to serve as foster parents, and possibly adopt a sibling group.

Moving forward in our fostering journey we knew that together we would be doing all we could to make new happy memories memoires while the children in our care were clinging on to every last memory that they had of their biological parents.

Good or bad, memories are ours as long as we want them to stay with us. Just like our children, they too, have memories, and unfortunately, so many of them are ingrained in their minds and haunt them daily. As such, we are working to embrace their past and have each of the children journaling their good memories, as they fear they are losing those positive experiences with their birth parents. We have encouraged them to draw pictures, write words, and even story- tell their positive memories of their parents. The bad memories are the ones we are working through, trying to let process with the children process, and helping them navigate on how to store them long-term. With those memories can be the ultimate challenge as our special needs children escalate, explode, and flip their lids, displaying their anger for all to see.

As memory- makers, we are digging for treasure in their little souls every day working. Our goal is to help our kiddos build new, wonderful, happy memories of their youth. Taking pictures and posting them around the house provides is providing triggers of good memories. Memories of being safe, secure, and loved.

It was during the summer when the house was quiet, that I wondered where did our two girls (ages five5 and six6) had disappear to? I followed their soft little voices to the bathroom, and I heard, "More, it's not working," as the five-year-old in her swimsuit was is sitting in three inches of water. Her older sister was is frantically pouring generous amounts of iodized salt on her legs and /feet. The youngest stated, "Quickly, add more, it's not working yet."

Their pure excitement and confidence as they quickly began to splash the water on the legs and /feet as they opened up the second salt container with the small little table salt shaker positioned by the bathroom sink as at their last resort. I quietly stepped into the bathroom, sat down, and whispered, "What's going on?" The pure look of desperation set in as my daughter's legs and /feet were not becoming the mermaid tail the girls they were hoping for. The pure hope and faith for them both to become mermaids, even if it was for five minutes, was slowing fading.

What memories do you have from your childhood? This week I remembered a found memory of my childhood, and today I took action on that memory. Today, it's early March, cold and rainy. Almost freezing, a chill was in the air, and I wanted to warm up the house. How better to do so? Why not some homemade chocolate chip cookies? I quickly whipped up a batch and had them ready for when the children got home from school.

The smiles, the warm hugs, and the excitement from our five children were just the memories I was hoping for. We sat and, had a warm cookie and a nice cold glass of milk. Their smiles were contagious, their love was overflowing, and the cookie made a new, wonderful memory of coming home from school.

What if we all took the time to create those small moments of memories and create time? To go all-in every day knowing that if not today, maybe tomorrow?

Yes, I created a mess in making the cookies. But at the end of the afternoon, what a beautiful mess to have. Simply because, I have the ability and gift to clean up these messes and to transform these little minds with amazing memories for life.

Reflection

- What memories can you create for your child?
- What do you need to let go of to be all-in for God?
- What do you need to do to be more present in their everyday lives?

Prayer

Dear God, help me be all-in with You every day. Wipe away the doubts I have, wipe away my fears and sin. Help me walk in Your Word, helping those I come in contact with every day. Let us create powerful, fun, and loving memories. Thank You for all the blessings we have. Allow for my faith to be unwavering in challenging times, and may I remember to praise You in times of celebration. Amen.

32. Simply More to Love

By Tracy Loken Weber

" This is how we know that we love the children of God: by loving God and carrying out his commands."
(1 John 5:2, 2020, NIV)

The day had finally come.

After two years of fostering a sibling group, we had now reached their adoption day. We were so excited to adopt two girls and one boy and to be their forever family. Our home was full of family and friends who came from out-of-state to witness this momentous day. Our home was full of love. In the wee morning hours I remember our six-year-old looking up at me and simply saying, "Mommy, when can you and Daddy adopt more children? More children need to be saved. Just like you and Daddy saved us." Tears came to my eyes as I could see the Lord working in her little heart. This is a conversation we kept having as our children brought it up to us. My husband and I worked to keep

Simply Dedicated

our foster care and adoptive home study and license active knowing that when the time was right, we would look to add to our family.

Flash forward two years. I received an emergency call late on a Thursday afternoon, followed by three more calls asking for my husband and me to seriously consider a placement of two siblings that needed a forever home right away. The transition would happen quickly, and the adoption case manager needed to know by Friday morning at 8 a.m. If we said Yes, the oldest sibling would be joining our family on Monday. We quickly reviewed the case notes, and we said Yes. Now looking back, every day I praise the Lord that we said Yes to these precious two girls.

When we sat down with our three children to share the happy news, they were so excited to help other children. Their pure joy and love for another child they had never met was amazing to witness. They silently knew the pain of being in foster care and separated from their siblings. Just these two factors created a unique bond for all five of our children.

We quickly learned that this thirteen-old-sibling had bravely taken her removal into her own hands and refused at all costs to go back to the pre-adoptive home that she was placed in. When she arrived on Monday, I was quickly reminded of the typical "luggage" a child in foster care arrives with—a black trash bag and brown paper sack. She had a smaller overnight bag and one pillow. She was here, and she looked scared. This was all new to her. Thankfully our little dog Charlie was here to love on her right away.

As we sat at our dining room table and the short-term case manager went over paperwork, this child looked on as Charlie lay in her lap. The other children were at school as we showed her around the house and helped her to settle in to her room. As the children arrived home from school, our eight-year-old ran up to her and wrapped her loving arms around her. Love was welcoming her. A child who was once part of the foster care system was welcoming another. A silent bond was uniting two children together. That night we kept it simple and ordered pizza for dinner, followed by ice cream for dessert, which she was never allowed to have at her previous placement.

The next morning, our new foster daughter asked when her little sister would join us. At that time, her sister was five years old, and she had a burning desire to have her removed out of that home right away. I shared with her that we have a place for her sister to be with us and that we needed social services to take the lead and make this transition work. In the meantime, we had a one-hour weekend visit with her at a local fast food restaurant with a little play area. The love of these two sisters was evident, and we could see that they needed to be reunited. During these visits I could see firsthand the verbal abuse, sarcasm, and lack of nurturing the younger sister was receiving. I had a gut feeling that something wasn't right about this placement and was now seeing firsthand what the oldest sister was sharing with me at home. After two months, her five-year-old sister joined our family.

Over time many layers of neglect and abuse were shared. We learned how their cereal and milk was measured out, how the girls were subject to verbal abuse, how the adults ate in front of the television while the two sisters were made to eat in the kitchen by themselves, and so much more. We learned how both girls were made to stay locked in a county park pavilion until midnight until their foster parent was done with her work shift to take them home to bed. Their pre-adoptive home was abusing their family pets as well. Now that the girls were under our roof, healing of the personal traumas they had both endured was beginning to take place both in our home and with their therapists.

As we welcomed them to our church family, the oldest wanted to volunteer in the nursery while our youngest children attended Sunday school classes. Together we are working to give them hope and something to believe it. Their healing continues to take place even though many questions followed, such as Where was God when I prayed for help? Why me? and Why do I have to be so different from other children?

After being in foster care for over five years and two homes later, both siblings had found their forever family. I have been told that we were different. Our oldest has stated many times that she can feel our love and how much we care about her and her sister. She even stated that we don't use our children for a "social status," and that we treat them as if they were our own children. At the age of thirteen, the oldest went shopping for the first time ever to pick out her own clothes. Yes, life really did change for both of these girls.

The girls were ready to be adopted, and the youngest put this down as her number one Christmas wish list item for Santa: She wanted to be adopted for Christmas. When the permanency hearing was presented to the courts, I was asked to speak. I shared with the court how the youngest was asking Santa to be adopted for Christmas. At that moment the clerk let out an "Ah…," and the judge sat back in his chair and looked at me. He stated that if this is her wish, then let's make this little girl's Christmas wish come true. On December 23, both girls were adopted and welcomed into our family, with friends and family once again surrounding our family.

Our first Christmas together was especially wonderful. The girls were moved to tears of praise and thanksgiving. For the first time in their lives they shared that the gifts they received were gifts they actually had wanted, and in turn we received the best Christmas gift ever, two daughters. From the very beginning, both girls joined our family and hearts naturally. It was as if they were hand-picked by God to join our home and family. Being adopted means to them both that there's no more moving, that now after all these years they have a forever family that will always be there for them no matter what. In turn, I was taught how much more love we have to give.

Reflection

- How have you noticed you have more love to give?
- How have you made a difference in a child's life?
- What lessons have you learned from my child?

Prayer

Heavenly Father, thank You for the opportunity to serve as this child's caregiver. Help me be the best advocate for my child, showing my love for my child every day. Create moments of calm, peace, and quiet just to be fully present for our family and child. Let us remember what it was like to be a child again, and help us to create that space for the child(ren) in our care. Help our child be a child again. In Your Son's name I pray, Amen.

33. Simply Moving Mountains Through Faith in God

By Tracy Loken Weber

" Now faith is confidence in what we hope for and assurance about what we do not see."
Hebrews 11:1, NIV)

Daily life with a special needs child is definitely a journey like no other. Actually, until one lives day-in and day-out with a special needs child, one really doesn't truly understand the complexities of the journey and terrain a family travels on a daily basis.

It's day 16. Our six-year-old daughter has been in the mental hospital for 16 days now. In order for her to come home, we need to have a safety plan in place, and no one is returning my phone calls. It is now 9 a.m. I pick up the phone and start making the phone calls to yet again receive voicemail after voicemail after voicemail. Messages left, and I again am left waiting.

Now it's late afternoon, and one voicemail is finally returned. For a split second I am filled with hope and belief that this voice on the other side of the phone will be able to help our daughter, will be able to help me navigate wrap-around supportive services and more.

To my surprise, this person, having never met me or my daughter, came right out and said that she, our daughter, will never amount to anything: that our daughter will never read, and if she is able to read, it will never be above a second-grade level. She went on to state that our daughter would need my support the rest of my life and that our daughter would never hold a job. Her lack of faith, her voice of judgment, and her incredible forceful attitude of knowing it all really blew my mind. I could hardly get a word in as her judgments continued to pour out.

My mind began to race…no reading, no employment, no real potential to become anything. I must find resources. I must be part of the change. I must begin to seek out how we can break down the medical and mental health silos. My notes become more detailed, change must happen not only for my child but also for all the other parents and children that are struggling every single day.

The peaks and valleys as we hike through our daily lives can sometimes be very treacherous. As you go about your daily life, ready to hike your way to the summit (daily goals/task list) you face the adventure—the day ahead—with enthusiasm and a can-do spirit. Although there are often unexpected phone calls, work plans change, behavioral outbursts occur, a flat tire happens, or even a child falls ill, and all of a sudden you have a setback that wasn't scheduled.

Oftentimes that setback leads to being late for an appointment or not being able to keep it at all. When this happens, your family is often penalized by the healthcare field for a "no-show" appointment, even when you call to explain that there is a mental health crisis occurring, there always seems to be a "cold" response, having your child being placed on the end of the waiting list, having yet again to wait months for their appointment time to be rescheduled. Even so, you are only allowed three "no shows" before you are dismissed from receiving medical services. Yet another system policy that needs a serious review.

That set-back alone could last a week or longer and that is when you fall back, you retreat and lean on God for faith and strength.

Sometimes our "base weight" full of our "hiking gear," or daily life, is more than you can bear. From therapy, to doctors' appointments, some weeks it just never ends. On average, our family has a minimum of twenty hours of professional support a week for our children. At times of feeling overwhelmed, I turn to God in prayer. He hears what is on our hearts and knows where we need the most support. God is ready to take on our base weight and our burdens. He is always there for you during the deepest valleys and the highest peaks. God is there to help you get to the summit of your daily goals and ultimate summit of heaven.

Reflection

- How can you advocate for your child more?
- What "base weight" do you need help with?

- What "mountains" do you need to help move?
- How can you advocate for overall medical changes for my child?
- What "base weight" do you need to unload to your daily life be more in line with God's Word and help you simplify my life?

Prayer

Dear Lord, when my days are overflowing and I feel as if I'm carrying more than I can, help me remember that You are always there to help me carry my "base weight" of daily life burdens. Help me slow down and make time for You, to make time for your Word, and to let the Holy Spirit to work in me. Amen.

34. Simply Opening Your Heart to a Child's Family

By Kevin and Jenny Poston

"Make my joy complete by being like-minded, having the same love, being one in spirit, and of one mind. Do nothing out of selfish ambition or vain conceit. Rather, in humility value others above yourselves, not looking to your own interests but each of you to the interests of the others."
Philippians 2:2-4, NIV)

One of the biggest apprehensions about being a foster parent is falling in love with a child and then having to give them back to their biological parents and never seeing them again.

But...what if you could continue to have a relationship with that child AND her family...even after reunification?

Sometimes with the right foundation laid, and God's blessing, that's just what happens. We did not go into foster care expecting to build lasting relationships with the bio family. God had other plans! In our initial training, there was lots of talk about the importance of building relationships with biological parents and words like "co-parenting" that really opened our eyes to the importance of the child's biological family to that young child. But, we had no idea where to begin; and we were nervous about what that would look like and if it would even work.

Our first long-term placement was a baby girl DEARLY loved by her mom and grandma. Little by little, through many visits, phone calls, texts, pictures, church services we invited them to, and holidays we celebrated together, we built trust and friendship. God was working on all of us to open our hearts to each other, for the good of the little one we all loved. That child always knew she was loved by her mom and grandma and also by us, and she also knew her mom and grandma were respected and appreciated by us.

Thankfully, the biological mom continued to work on the conditions the agency gave her, and though it took much longer than she wanted, on Valentine's Day 2017, all her hard work paid off as she got to take her little girl home with her to stay. Reunification was such a joy-filled and blessed day! But would this be the end of our contact with them?

Her mom said no, it would not. She thanked us for never judging her despite her challenges, and for loving her daughter while also respecting her own love for her daughter. She recognized that her daughter had a unique and deep relationship with us and that it would only be a blessing to encourage that relationship to continue.

That adorable baby girl has now grown into a beautiful, inquisitive, spunky preschooler who knows us as her godparents. We see her, mom, and grandma frequently and we speak with them on the phone often, and still offer each other support and love as much as ever. Most importantly, we still have the opportunity to share Jesus with her and her family.

What did we learn? When possible, support the child's relationships with their family, and you just might find they come to consider you like part of the family.

What if you could continue to have a relationship ... even after reunification?

Reflection

- How can you increase positive connections between your child's biological family and you?
- How can you show your child you understand the importance of their biological family in their life?
- How can you show them it's Jesus' love for you that moves you to love them?

Prayer

Dear Father of the fatherless, as you opened your heart to seek a relationship with me, so now open my heart to any opportunities to build relationships with the family of children in my care, for the blessing of those children, and the eternal growth of your kingdom. In my brother Jesus' name. Amen.

35. Simply Paperwork

By Julie P. Watson

"Whatever you do, work at it with all your heart, as working for the Lord, not for human masters, since you know that you will receive an inheritance from the Lord as a reward. It is the Lord Christ you are serving."
(Colossians 3:23-24, NIV)

Paperwork, paperwork. When does it ever end? If you're a new foster parent or preparing to become one, I feel for you—there is a lot of paperwork to deal with!

It wasn't that long ago I was buried in paperwork preparing to become a certified foster parent. It was a stressful time, but it was expected. I knew what was expected of me. I knew what our deadlines were and who to ask if, by chance, we needed a little more time. The great thing on the front end of this is you can almost take as long as you want — you just don't get any children placed in your home until you finish every last requirement! However, I don't think I truly realized how much paperwork there would be after the placement (or how time-intensive it would be).

I wasn't prepared for the list of required monthly foster forms I needed to complete for my children—all THREE children! That's right, when you accept a sibling set, you get to double, triple, even quadruple your paperwork every month you foster. (Don't forget other entities such as medical paperwork, school registrations, and summer camps). Thankfully, our intent was to adopt from the beginning, so when it started I could see the light at the end of the tunnel… or could I?

We were originally told our case should be in front of an adoption judge within nine months. Ah, music to my ears! But, no, that wasn't the case at all. Try twenty-one months later, we finally graced the judge's courtroom to finalize our adoption. And what a crazy rollercoaster ride it was! Ah, but back to the paperwork.

There were several laborious reports due every month for each child. Among those I least liked were the monthly clothing counts and monetary allowance records (names for each of these forms are likely to vary, so I'll keep them general). Honestly, I hated the end of each month when I had to wash and fold all the kids' clothes just so I could count every single article of clothing. Seriously, isn't it just important that the children have at least a week's worth of clothing and leave it at that? Oh no, we had to count everything…every shirt (long-sleeved and short-sleeved counted separately), pants, shorts, pajamas, pair of underwear, pair of socks (even those missing a pair), etc.

Now, at one point my oldest son had thirty-six pairs of socks! My daughter had twenty-four pairs of underwear and thirty-two dresses (she came to us owning three, so having this many was our fault as well as those that lavished her with new or gently used hand-me-down gowns). The children came to us without owning even one swimsuit. By the third month they had three swimsuits each! They had also accumulated slippers, robes, belts, hats, scarves, gloves, snow-jackets and additional general clothing. Counting their clothing each month became a chore I began to loathe. I dreamt of the day they would finally be ours so this clothes-counting nightmare could come to an end!

The monthly monetary allowance record was another frustrating one. Why? Because at age five you are required to start giving your foster child a weekly allowance equal to their age—WHETHER OR NOT they do anything to earn it! This was a source of contentment for me because I was required to do it, but when I was a child, I received an allowance only if I earned it. What this caused with my kids was a huge amount of entitlement. Not only did I have to pay them, I had to allow them to spend a portion of it as well. Financial literacy is highly important to me. God told us to be good stewards of the things He entrusted to us, and I had a hard time teaching that concept to two five-year-olds who came to me more entitled than average American teenagers!

Let's briefly discuss the entitlement issues with some foster kids (clearly this doesn't apply to them all). The first Christmas we experienced with our three darlings ages six, five, and four by Christmastime, was epic, and not in a good way. They had been given twenty presents each from numerous sources. It took us over four hours to open all the gifts! There was so much, and they were so overwhelmed by it all, their eyes were glossed over by the end of the day. But, the real kicker here: At the end of opening their gifts, they genuinely asked us if that was it or if there was more! I was in utter shock! Never had I seen that kind of entitlement in such young children. They barely even remembered what they had just opened unless it was a favorite gift. I have a few other entitlement stories I could share, but I'll spare you. Just be prepared!

We learned much from those early experiences. I'm happy to say that as of our adoption year, Christmas gifts follow a new tradition: four gifts each, plus one family gift. On Christmas Eve they receive a gift "from Jesus" (usually a Bible, devotional, or prayer journal), then on Christmas Day they receive three gifts, named after the gifts of the wisemen who visited young Jesus: a "Gold" gift (their big ticket item: expensive toy, new bike, etc.), a "Frankincense" gift (new clothing or books they want), and lastly, a "Myrrh" gift (something to spark their creativity: lego building books, lighted drawing pads, DIY projects, etc.). The family gift follows a theme for each year. For instance, the first year doing this our family theme was "better communication." The gift we opened together was a CB radio and walkie talkies. We then created games to foster better communication. One example was that a person at the CB radio base would have to communicate to the others using walkie talkies on how to find an object hidden in their room without anything other than one-word directions (hot/cold, left/right, up/down, etc.). The children always remember their gifts now! They maintain special memories at Christmastime, they've grown substantially in their faith, and we have grown much closer as a family.

Back to paperwork... another monthly form I detested was the injury/incident report required for any cut or bruise over a quarter inch in length. Honestly, with two very active boys, this became almost a daily occurrence! During the first two years, their school nurse had my phone number on speed dial. I became so familiar with her, we were on a first-name basis by the end of week two of the first year. Don't get me wrong, I understood the purpose of these forms, but they became monotonous and, during stressful times, downright overwhelming.

Thank God these forms all went away on month twenty-two for us, but if you're in the thick of them, just know there is a purpose for each. Your sacrifice is appreciated by those who've gone before you, as well as your children. Hopefully, one day in the future they will come to appreciate what you did for them, just as we appreciate what God has done for us. And, if you're adopting like we did, there is a light at the end of the tunnel. Just keep going, God is with you; you can do this!

Reflection

Ever heard the quote, "the devil is in the details?" Well, there is some truth to that, but often details are required. Guess what? God is there too, helping you to get through all the things required to do this very important job. Foster parents play a vital role in the lives of the children who become a part of their family. Kids need to learn to trust adults, see how a real family operates, heal from the pain and losses they have endured, all while still in the midst of living it. Ministering to these precious kiddos is a blessing more to you than you'll ever realize—but the eternal rewards far outweigh the frustrations of completing tedious monthly reports.

Prayer

Dear Jesus, I know You placed me in this position to minister to children in need, and I heartily do that. But Lord, sometimes the work is overwhelming and stressful. Please help me to remember the reason I am here, the purpose You have given me, and the lives I am impacting by modeling Your love. I know You will get me through this, and You will be glorified through it all!

Simply Dedicated

Thank You, Lord, for knowing what's in our best interest and how we can serve You with a joyful heart, even in the tedious. I love You! Amen

36. Simply A Parent

By Kim S Bushey, A Fellow Handmaiden

"Fear of man will prove to be a snare."
(Proverbs 29:25a, NIV)

Self-Control, my daughter, suffers from enuresis. No one told me when we got her. Of course, it did not take long to figure this out. I thought, perhaps, this is a response to all the change that has just happened; it is fear from being in a new place. However, as time went on and many wet beds later, I realized this was more than that, perhaps this was trauma based.

I began to research ways that I could help and that's when I discovered the word enuresis, otherwise known as bedwetting. How could I reassure this precious child that I was there for her and we would get through this? I could tell her that it happens to lots of children and even adults; and I would comfort her and myself.

We always made sure a light was on at night, or more than one, including a night light, a closet light, sometimes the room light itself, and the bathroom light. I checked "lights" off the list of things tried. We got plastic mattress protectors and encouraged some more. We Checked that off the list as well. We bought a special device which is an arm band and a little device that connects to the undergarments to detect any moisture to alarm the child and parent it's time to use the bathroom, because maybe Self-Control is just a very deep sleeper, although I wasn't so sure of that, I could now check that off the "help" list as well. We trained her on how to use the new device, day after day. We got new batteries. We trained again and again on how to use it, getting up night after night to no avail. We checked all of that off the impervious list of "how to help".

After many months that turned into more than a year of nothing helping and a lot of hidden "accidents" later, we had the dreaded talk about "pull-ups" for bedtime. The child was a bit older, so this was not a welcome thought; in her word's "pullups are for babies". While there was as much positive reaffirmation, the pull-ups still ended up wet and hidden in all sorts of places, until I would smell them out of course. It was like a "game" of hide and sniff.

As the years went by, and several mattress sets, stained and smelly carpet and closet floors later, I began to get weary. I was not so sure this was really fear, trauma, deep sleep, or a medical issue. I researched again to reassure myself I could help her through this. It was really an issue and not just laziness, but that is what I thought: maybe just maybe, she just didn't want to get up at night. I had been patient, kind, loving, reassuring, but I had also gotten weary over the years.

Simply Dedicated

My husband and I had to figure out how to put in an egress window on the lower level just so we could add another bedroom. All the girls in the house refused to sleep in the same room with Self-Control because of the issue at hand. There were times over the years when it seemed like we'd "conquered" the trouble, but it came back. It was exhausting. We tried to help our child understand that "bacteria can grow in places from hiding wet garments and sheets."

I felt like we'd tried everything. What was I doing wrong? I read books. I took all the blame because of the times when I felt angry. This all went on for years. We moved to a new house and the problem seemed to disappear altogether; but no, it was just being hidden and my nose began to sniff it out. I had been lied to again and again. The mattress protectors were hidden in the closet under clothes. The pull-ups were in the package unworn. The new carpet was soaked because it had gone through the mattress and the box spring. The lights were on. The alarm had long been forgotten. The bedrooms had to be rearranged again, it never seemed to happen during the night when I was waking myself up to wake her up but, in the morning, and this mom was done.

Just once more I asked Self-Control again, why? This time, however, came the real answer. "I just don't feel like getting up in the morning, I'm tired." I was speechless. I was angry. I knew it. I know without a doubt there are people who really have a medical challenge with enuresis, it's a real thing, however in my spirit for years I thought this "I don't feel like it" was the real problem. BUT, I just could not bring myself to admit it. I was afraid to tell the social worker initially, later I was afraid to tell the doctor. How could I think that she might just be lazy? It was inconceivable.

I was an awful parent for thinking it and I knew it. Now, here she was saying it to my face. We had a little bit of "loud fellowship" that day. We worked on this whole, "I just don't feel like getting up" thing for a while, even months. We had an appointment at the doctor's office sometime later and while there I brought up this "enuresis" trouble we were having at the end of the visit because the doctor had asked if there was anything else we'd like to talk about.

The doctor, being the good physician she is, began to reassure my daughter that lots of people have this trouble and she would eventually outgrow it. Then she asked me if I'd made sure she had a light just in case Self-Control had any issue with fear of the dark. I began the very long litany of measures we've taken over the past five plus years in helping our daughter and then ended with the comments my daughter herself had said when she told me she just didn't feel like getting up. The doctor stopped. Turned to my teen and said in a nice firm voice, "That is your responsibility, you have to get up and use the bathroom."

That was the end of it! All the years, the mattress sets, mattress protectors, the laundry, the moving bedrooms around, the lights, the pull ups, alarms, books, egress window, all of it was done with one simple firm statement from the doctor. She never wet the bed again. I sure was glad I finally told someone even though I may seem like the "bad mom" for thinking such a thing about my child. Lazy.

While this child does have other issues that are complicated and need help, I thought for a long time "enuresis" was not one of them, turns out, I was right.

Reflection

I confided in a godly woman one afternoon some of the troubles burdening my heart. I told her I was "afraid" to just be a parent sometimes. Afraid because of past experiences with social workers, afraid because of lies spoken to people by my own children, afraid of what others would think, afraid of my own failures of attempting to be "the best" parent , just plain afraid I'd never measure up to all I should be. I cried. She replied with the simplest of statements. "Wouldn't it be nice to just parent without fear."

In my heart there was a resounding YES! I let those words sink deep into my soul. I thought about them, scripture came to my mind over and over to back them up. I HAD to parent without fear. I could no longer be snared. My foot had been set free from the trap. I was incredibly grateful for the simple comment of a much younger mom and I applied that wisdom. Yes, I do it wrong sometimes. I yell at my kids. I get tired. I am not always a godly example. I sneak chocolate in my closet. I get weary from doing well and I cry. I need help. I need breaks because I just cannot take it anymore. While I do all this, yet I deeply love my children. I ask for forgiveness. I would NOT want to go through this life without them, ever. I am a parent. I am here, loving, cooking, cleaning, teaching, caring, playing. I am here with them and I choose to do it without fear of what others think.

Are we still "judged" and do people tell us what they think? Sure they do! Will they ever walk in my shoes to see what it is really like? I doubt it, so they can talk all they want because they will be held accountable for every empty word they speak.

> "But I tell you that everyone will have to give account on the day of judgment for every empty word they have spoken."
> Matthew 12:36 NIV

- How can you parent without fear?
- How would this impact your family?

Prayer

Lord Jesus, thank you for helping me to just be a parent. Thank you for all the opportunities to grow and thank you for heavenly comfort for growing pains, and for chocolate. I love you Lord, and I want to be like you, help me. Please forgive me for having the fear of man. I do not want to be snared by the enemy like that. You are so good and faithful to forgive and I am so thankful I can walk in Your peace. If I am tempted, I know you will always give me a way out; help me to remember to ask for it. I can't do this without you and I certainly don't want to. "Bless the Lord oh my soul and forget not all his benefits" (Psalm 103:2 ESV). AMEN

37. Simply Planned

By Erica R. Johnsrud

" 'For I know the plans I have for you,' declares the LORD, 'plans to prosper you and not to harm you, plans to give you hope and a future' "

(Jeremiah 29:11, NIV).

Face down in a pool of my tears, on our laminate bedroom floor, I begged God to help me—I am completely unhinged—put me out of my misery now! Strong arms lifted me up off the floor and carefully placed me onto the bed. A pair of concerned blue eyes stared at me. One had a ring of gold that I focused on. My husband whispered, "We're done with this. It's not worth it. I hate seeing you like this." The year-long toll of the daily chores of tracking my temperature, ovulation and periods, ovulation and pregnancy tests, doctor's appointments, and fertility treatments had finally consumed us. The hormonal roller coaster of infertility had to end soon, before it derailed my sanity. Pair that with questions of friends, family, coworkers, and acquaintances like, "When are you having kids?" or "Are you pregnant yet?" or ridiculously obvious statements like "You aren't getting any younger!"

I didn't think I could take it anymore. It took awhile, but I realized I was depressed. For months now, I had come up with excuses to not stay long or not even attend my friends' children's birthday parties, or playdates. It physically pained me to see all of their children when I couldn't conceive. I longed for children. Every job I ever had since I was twelve revolved around children: babysitter, nanny, day care provider, instructor, coach, teacher—even as the birthday clown at Hardees in my teen years. I had many students over the years that I called my kids; I had made children my life, but I had none of my own to care for at home. That's how our adoption journey began. Well, almost.

I had my life all planned out as a teenager: graduate college, establish a teaching career, get married, have two birth children, and then adopt a toddler from another country.

Phases one and two were checked off at age twenty-two. The third phase was checked off at age thirty. My husband and I added a phase "3.1"—a 5-year "us time" before we would start having children. For phase four in my life plan, I did everything perfectly: saw my doctor for advice on going off the pill; got on prenatal vitamins and folic acid to prepare a healthy environment and prevent neural tube defects; cut out the occasional alcohol, caffeine, acetaminophen, cough drops, etc. I was determined to have the healthiest pregnancy ever. Heck, we even had everything a child needed for the first few years of life. When my friends knew we were in "trying" mode—who am I kidding? even before—they started sending over more clothes and kids' items. My friends each had a boy and a girl, and claimed to be done having children. Most of the clothes would go from friend to friend to friend, and then end up with us, where we created this giant shrine to the children we didn't even have yet. It was all stacked in plastic totes in a corner of our garage. In the words of Chandler from my favorite sitcom, "Could we be more prepared?"

"The heart of man plans his way, but the Lord establishes his steps"
(Proverbs 16:9).

Becoming foster parents was something we talked about, but decided it wasn't for us. We knew we'd need to have a foster license to adopt, but as teachers in an area where a disproportionate amount of students have been in foster care, and being mandated reporters whose reports often are part of the process of putting a child in the foster care system, I knew it wasn't something I could do. Family reunification is the ultimate goal, especially on reservations, but all too many times I would have students start acting out at the end of the day, especially the end of the week, and they'd confide in me. I would have to make the report to social services, and I'd be told to send the child home on the bus. Believe me, several times I have seriously considered having the student "miss" the bus or take them to my house, and many have asked me, begged me, to do just that. Worse yet, some would shrug their shoulders as if it was nothing, hug me as if to reassure me that it was okay to send them home to their abusers. Nope, doing foster care would ultimately end with me in jail, because I'd refuse to send the child home if I thought they were in danger. No, we definitely will NOT do foster care.

Simply Dedicated

"Many are the plans in the mind of a man, but it is the purpose of the Lord that will stand"
(Proverbs 19:21).

A couple of years before I got married, a mentoring program, Kinship, was started, and I was excited to sign up! I was paired with an adorable five-year-old girl, Jayleigh (not her real name). Every week for the next eight years I would spend time with Jayleigh. We'd do crafts. We'd do crafts, bake, go to the movies and parks, and take short trips to the North Shore to see waterfalls and Lake Superior, and the headwaters of the Mississippi, and to my in-laws' farm. Even after the program was no longer active, we continued to spend time together. We had a special role for her at our wedding: pass out the wedding bubbles. When Jayleigh was about thirteen, she stopped taking my calls. Yes, she was now a teenager, but was still a big part of our family, and I couldn't help think there was more to being brushed off by her than just being a teenager! I found out Jayleigh's mom was back in her life. Later Jayleigh told me that she stopped spending time with me, because she knew I wouldn't approve of the "activities" she did with her mom. Jayleigh had a tumultuous upbringing: domestic violence, abuse, drugs, alcohol—more than a child should have to worry about. Her father was in prison, and her mother was in and out of her life, in and out of jail, and in and out of treatment, leaving Jayleigh and her siblings to live with her grandma, who tried to do right by her grandchildren, but it was a lot for such a frail woman.

When Jayleigh was fifteen, we found out that she was at the youth shelter, and had voluntarily left her home—she wanted to get out, away from that life. After praying, and frankly not much discussion, we knew that we needed to take her in. We got an emergency foster license, and said we would be her foster parents for the next three years until she graduated. Jayleigh, a shy young lady, for as long as I could remember, had always taken care of her sisters and family. Despite her upbringing, her special needs, and her brain differences, she was strong and resilient. It was her time to be taken care of. We wanted to allow her to be a child, and not have to worry about adult problems for as long as possible. Jayleigh and her grandma both agreed to let her live with us. Our foster license was expedited as an emergency license, and Jayleigh moved in.

We learned a lot from Jayleigh, especially about the power of loyalty to one's birth family, regardless of how many adverse childhood experiences one endured while living with them. We only had Jayleigh a few months. The contact with her family, including her mother who would hang out near the school each morning and offer Jayleigh and her friends coffee and breakfast, filled her with guilt, as she shared how she was happy and thriving. Eventually she was torn between two worlds, and decided to leave them both behind, tried to run away, and ended up in residential treatment.

"Commit to the Lord whatever you do, and he will establish your plans"
(Proverbs 16:3).

After Jayleigh, we were ready to get back to our plan of adopting a child. The more we talked, we thought, why only one? Sibling groups are so much harder to place, why not two or three at once?

As anyone in the waiting children (from the foster system) world of adoption knows, it is a world of hurry up and wait! Hurry up and write your bio, collect all of your financial statements, get your home study done, get your home inspected, have your criminal background checked, attend foster care classes, and…wait. While waiting some more during the matching process, I tried to keep myself busy with more reading about hurt children, and journaling (incidentally in a journal Jayleigh got me for Christmas when she was ten) for my faith walk. My husband and I discussed how we don't hear God, and probably miss all of His signs. We joked that we needed a big ol' flashing neon sign. As I look back to my journal, I read that one of my biggest fears was that we were going to be so eager to be matched with children, that we might not listen to God and it be the wrong one, and we may consider disrupting the adoption. I could not imagine doing that, but I know that it happens. I prayed and then opened my Bible. The first verse I laid my eyes upon was Psalm 113:9, "He settles the childless woman in her home as a happy mother of children. Praise the Lord." (NIV).

"He settles the childless woman in her home as a happy mother of children. Praise the Lord" (Psalm 113:9).

That was quick! Well played, God, well played! He spoke; I heard; my fear calmed.

We submitted a home study for a sibling pair of girls and were contacted by the girls' two adoption workers. They usually narrow the home studies down to five to seven to interview. I guess each worker took half a stack and then switched. When they met back, each had

Sitting at a round table in a small room in the county human services building, I realized this room is where we would have our final collateral meeting before knowing for sure if these girls were going to be ours. The start of our family begins here. Little did I know, this same room was the location of our girls' final visit with their birth mom. One of the workers asked, "Would you like to see a picture of your girls?" With all of the other children we had submitted home studies for, there was always a picture. We didn't even know what our girls looked like—the poor quality of a black and white copy that was faxed didn't really help much. The worker took out a wallet photo and slid it across the table. My eyes welled with tears, and I whispered, "They're beautiful!" God made these girls for us.

The beautiful brown-eyed girls of ours came home with us for good a few months later. We finally got our children! Has it been easy? No, not for any of us. Our gain is inevitably someone's loss. Are we perfect parents? Far from it, but we keep learning. I've certainly learned a lot about faith, hope, and patience, and of course giving up a little control. I waver, but I always come back.

"And we know that in all things God works for the good of those who love him, who have been called according to his purpose"
(Romans 8:28 NIV).

Even when you think God's ultimate Plan for you has been laid out, and your prayers, no matter what or how long, have been answered— He might surprise you with the fluidity of His Plan, and open a door you thought had been closed. He might take that proverbial lemon in your life and make you the sweetest lemonade. How do I know this? Because as I sit here writing this final paragraph, almost ten years later after being blessed with our two precious daughters, I rock an adorable seven-month-old baby girl that we have the honor of raising; but that, my friends, is another chapter in another book, after God has decided to finish laying out His Plan for us.

"I didn't give you the gift of life; life gave me the gift of you."-unknown

Reflection

"The heart of man plans his way, but the Lord establishes his steps"
(Proverbs 16:9).

- How would your life look like if you don't slow down, and trust in God's timing?
- What are other areas in your life that you need to give up control, and truly trust in God?
- How will you be mindful of your temptation to act upon your own will, ways, and worries?

Prayer

Dear Lord, I know at times I try to hold onto control of the things that I think I can. I do things my way, in my time, causing me to lose sight of You. I need to trust that You are preparing amazing things for me. Help me to slow down, be patient, and trust in Your perfect timing. Guide me to be still and remember you are God, and keep you present. In Jesus' name, Amen.

38. Simply Pooped

By Julie P. Watson

"Come to me, all you who are weary and burdened, and I will give you rest. Take my yoke upon you and learn from me, for I am gentle and humble in heart, and you will find rest for your souls. For my yoke is easy and my burden is light."

(Matthew 11:28-30, NIV)

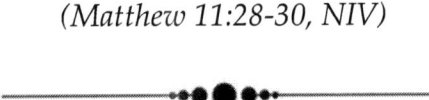

If you're currently a foster parent, then you are very aware of your present energy levels. They're probably hovering somewhere on the low end of an ascending one-to-ten scale. If you haven't yet received your first placement, then you're in for a real energy drain. Trust me, you'll soon be quite pooped—and that will be the understatement of the decade!

Beyond being pooped physically, you will be pooped emotionally, mentally, relationally, and even spiritually to some degree. You will be exhausted on top of being tired on top of being pooped. And, it will be that way for quite some time, depending on the age(s) and number of children in your placement.

We were blessed with a sibling set of three kiddos ages five, five and three. The bonus in that setup was that the two oldest were less than thirty days apart and in constant competition for attention, affection, and overall hierarchy in the family. My daughter, being the younger of the two, constantly wished (and acted like) she was the eldest. She came to us extremely parentified ("parent-like"). In fact, I had never met such a parentified child in my life. She was five going on fifteen, and in a lot of ways she scared me while also exhausting me in the process of learning age-appropriate behaviors! The first thing I had to teach her was how to be (and act like) a child. Honestly, to this day, I am still working on that one. Once children lose their childhood, it is quite the undertaking to get it back—or create one at the very least. The power struggle is real!

Behaviors that continually exhaust include the usuals: tantrums, power struggles, sibling rivalries, attention-seeking, back-talking, general disobedience, selective listening, lying, stealing, night terrors, poor sleep overall, eating battles, and, last but certainly not least, potty problems. Being pooped becomes a massive double entendre when you bring in potty problems. Nope, sadly, I'm not joking one bit.

We have encountered more than our share of toilet drama, and, unfortunately, it did not end with one of our children in the earlier years, as one would expect. We recently underwent another battle with our eleven-year-old son at the beginning of this year. It took me by complete shock! We now refer to this period as #PoopGate. I've dealt with a lot of poop over the past six years, but this last bout was POOP GALORE!

All these behaviors are exhausting, whether they're new or repeated. Having to wipe the rear-end of an eleven-year-old and use diaper ointment on him because he had developed a rash simply by sitting in his own feces, was less than enjoyable. And hearing why he did it—because he didn't want to poop at school using their rough toilet paper—became even more frustrating and exhausting! This child has Fetal Alcohol Syndrome (FAS) and he literally does not have the ability to see cause and effect of his choices. He has permanent brain damage, and all we can do is teach him time and again how to properly use the toilet, correcting new, inappropriate, and unpleasant habits.

Thankfully, the last time he had a serious problem was when he was seven. He would hold his poop in (much like this last time) and then have accidents in his pants at school. At one point he didn't have a bowel movement for nine days straight. When he finally did have one, it was GREEN! It scared us half to death, and we rushed him to the doctor. The doctor reassured us this was more common than we realized and gave us steps to assist our son. Our son received stool softeners for about six months and wore pull-ups until he understood how to control his body. He had to learn what it physically felt like inside his body when he needed to evacuate his bowels.

Reality check on this… you literally have to place your hand on the child's abdomen to explain exactly where they will begin to feel pressure in their gut when they have to poop. For those who have littles (toddlers who need to be potty trained), this is an expected parental duty for that age group. But children in foster care can have potty problems at every age because they may have never had proper parenting instruction, along with so many other missed needs. You often parent backwards developmentally, in order to get them developmentally caught up. Reaching milestones that should have been reached beforehand are important to celebrate for yourself as well as with your child(ren).

Back to my son... even through all the clean up (which this last time included poop all over his room—don't ask), God knew we would go through this. It was no surprise to Him, even though we continue to be surprised six years into this parenting adventure. God also knew, as tired as we would become, He would provide His supernatural strength for us to lean on and rejuvenate ourselves just to make it through each day. Thankfully, my son got through this bout quickly and bounced back to healthy bowels and habits.

This was all in God's plans for us. He wanted to teach us patience, compassion, and understanding to children who hadn't received the vital nurturing needed in those early years. Difficult things will continue to show up in our kids' lives as they age up. All we can do is lean on the One who created these children, and refill our cups of comfort and strength, continually resting at the feet of our Savior. He loves these kids, and so do we, so we journey onward and upward, pooped or not.

Reflection

Throughout your fostering and/or adoption journey, prayers for strength and energy are mandatory on a daily basis just to get through it all. God is not surprised by the struggles you'll face, but if He brought you to this, then He certainly will bring you through it. He is your most important partner in this journey as you and your spouse will often experience exhaustion at the same time. You will each need to go to God in those moments so you don't mistakenly take things out on each other. The greatest gift you can give to one another during this journey is agreeing ahead of time to stand in unity no matter what.

Prayer

Heavenly Father, You already know everything we will endure on this journey. We pray for peace about all the unknowns regarding our child(ren). No matter what happens, You will guide us through the tough things, the unpleasant things, the things which exhaust us, and especially those that try to divide us. Please help us to always keep You at the center—You are the partner we will lean on time and time again. We pray for Your supernatural strength and wisdom as we overcome every challenge. Thank You for Your presence in this journey with us, guiding our steps, keeping us on Your lighted path of truth always. In Jesus's name we pray, Amen!

39. Simply Practice Self-Care

By Erica R. Johnsrud

"but those who hope in the LORD will renew their strength. They will soar on wings like eagles; they will run and not grow weary, they will walk and not be faint" (Isaiah 40:31, NIV).

Being a mom isn't easy. Being a mom of a special needs child isn't easy. Being a mom of a child with a very traumatic history isn't easy. Being a mom of a child with special needs and a traumatic history isn't easy. Adopting TWO children from foster care with...I'll stop; you get the picture. Or maybe you don't. In fact, most probably don't get it, unless you are one of these parents or a professional who works with these families like mine, or do a lot of reading and research on these subjects. Otherwise, how would you? One thing that I have learned to accept is that most people outside of these circles do not understand because they do not get to see the struggles that we go through on a daily basis. You probably don't want to. Many families who have children with these "life resumes" don't necessarily give you the hairy details of what

Simply Dedicated

this is like. We can't. We may attempt, but more often than not, we stop. We soon realize we are on our own island. I am a glass-half-full kind of person, so I am grateful we have an island, but yet we are drowning. I admit, sometimes I talk too much and share more than I should. My children have given me permission to share if it helps other children and families like ours. It has helped me work with students and families in similar situations for my job as a teacher.

Don't get me wrong, there are many caring people who want to help, want to listen, want to learn, but many don't understand. There are some that don't understand so much that they judge, or reject what they don't understand, or worse yet tell you all kinds of advice about how to parent: "If she were my child, I'd..." or even worse yet, "Guess you didn't know what you were getting into!" Is this helpful? Of course not, but, I've learned to take a deep breath and ask, what is worth my time and emotions at that moment? I can choose to use the moment to educate or I can decide the person isn't going to really understand, and move on with my day. The good news is that either decision can be healthy!

No wonder whenever we get together with professionals or families like ours who "get it," it is as if we are given a raft so we can leave that lonely island of ours, even if only for a small period of time, before the overwhelming waves send us crashing back to our island of reality. People who "get it," we love you! People who "get it," we need you, in fact we crave you! You don't look at us as if we are strange when we let slip that our nine-year-old drinks from a sippy cup while we swaddle her and rock her to sleep because she missed out on nurturing critical for "normal" development before she came to us. You don't look at us strangely when you see our strategically placed notes and visuals such as: If you are up before 6 a.m., stay in your room unless (visuals showing bathroom, fire, medical emergencies, etc), accompanied by a list of appropriate activities to do in one's room until others wake up (as opposed to standing over us while we sleep, waiting "patiently" until we wake up, or just plain waking us up!) or visuals showing your teenager that Pull-ups/ pads go in the garbage as opposed to under furniture, on the floor, stuffed in the back of the closet, or in the toilet. In fact, you probably will share similar stories, and we'll laugh together about them. Because if we do not share these crazy "normals" with someone else, we'll implode or explode! You nod your head with understanding when we explain how we are going to be late for the family Christmas dinner because our ten- (or twelve- or sixteen-) year-old is raging. You understand it's not a spoiled child tantrum. You understand that we are going to need time to let her finish letting out her pain, her fear, her anxiety, her anger, or her guilt of wanting to enjoy this holiday, but struggles with enjoying this new life, and feelings of disloyalty to the family that created her. You understand that we will need time to hold her and rock her and help her calm the emotional part of her brain, the amygdala. You understand that we may need to cancel our plans, because this all took too much of an emotional toll, on all of us, that we are "done" for the day. You understand that we "don't do chronological age" in our home. You don't say things like, "She's ___years old, she should/shouldn't be able to…"

10,.. wash her own hair

14,… stay home alone

15, …take drivers' training

16, ... drive

17, ...go hang out with her friends at the mall(without you being there)

18, ...do what she wants; she's an adult (Please, for the sake of your sanity, do NOT, I repeat, do NOT EVER tell your child with brain differences who are very literal thinkers that when they are eighteen they can do what they want. Especially if your child most likely will not be able to fully live on their own. Trust me, the repercussions can be catastrophic.)

You understand. Speaking of understanding, there are many things that I wish that I had understood, or at least didn't ignore as an adoptive mother. These mystical things really boil down to one: self-care. Yes, that can look like a relaxing bubble bath, a girls' night out, or perhaps more realistically, hiding in the bathroom, or pretending you are still sleeping for a few extra minutes. It may take some juggling. Okay,

maybe a lot of juggling, but even if you have to hire a mature teenager to come over to play with or hang out with your kids briefly while you are home so you can take a nap or do your Bible study, or yoga or whatever you want or need to do, it'll be worth it every now and then.

Self-care is a priority and a necessity—not a luxury.

Respite Care. Now that our girls are twenty and almost seventeen, we look back and realize that perhaps we should have utilized respite, although, it can be difficult to get in some rural communities, along with other supports. We originally did not utilize respite care, because our girls were sent to respite while in foster care, and never went back to some of the placements. We feared that our beautiful girls who struggled with attachment, would think that they weren't coming back to us, if they went to respite. We didn't want to stir up any more fear than necessary, and we knew that after coming back, there would be meltdowns or rages, but after a few years when they were feeling more secure, perhaps this would have been a good thing. Respite is good for the adults and children. We all need a break from each other sometimes, and that is okay.

> *"So do not fear, for I am with you; do not be dismayed, for I am your God. I will strengthen you and help you; I will uphold you with my righteous right hand"*
> *(Isaiah 41:10, NIV).*

Date nights. I wish we had had more of them. You and your spouse/significant other need your alone time too. We did not do many of these for a couple of reasons: We did not want to "use up" our favors with friends and family, and one of our girls especially would seem to sabotage our date nights, due to abandonment issues. Heck, my husband and I have "mini-dates" whenever possible. This is usually five minutes, here , ten minutes there. They eventually add up, right? Regardless, it is so important to have this time to connect or reconnect with your partner. It is also so positive for your children to see healthy relationships; many of them may not have experienced that in the past.

Simply Dedicated

"Be strong enough to stand alone, smart enough to know when you need help, and brave enough to ask for it."
Ziad K. Abdelnour

Support Systems (especially of people who "get it"). One of the best things we did was join our local adoption support group when we started the adoption process. We were able to hear everyone's stories (including horror stories!), celebrate the good things that happen no matter how small, get support on the things that didn't go so well, etc. We were able to ask many questions and get resources, and ideas for who were good therapists and other providers in the area. One couple we met at these meetings joked about how they "broke in" the therapists on the dynamics of adoption! Actually, that really wasn't a joke. Finding providers that understand trauma, disabilities, and adoption are essential, and adoption/foster support groups can be a wealth of local information. I have also found social media support groups to be helpful, and you don't have to wait for that once-a-month meeting to get your answers

What boosts your mood and fuels your soul? Run, dance, walk, sing, meditate, pray! If you are in need of counseling, reach out. Caregiver burnout and compassion fatigue are real things, and they are not good for anyone. Sometimes we as caregivers of children (even adult children) with special needs feel guilty that we need a break. Parenting these children requires more attention, more patience, more compassion, more stressors—and more rewards. We have our own unique revolving set of tools in our tool box, and using them can be exhausting. Regardless of your situation, it is imperative to practice self-care, not only for you (because self-care is NOT selfish) but for your children. You probably have to model and practice many things for your children, why not taking care of yourself? Your children are worth it, and so are you!

"Come to me, all you who are weary and burdened, and I will give you rest. Take my yoke upon you and learn from me, for I am gentle and humble in heart, and you will find rest for your souls. For my yoke is easy and my burden is light."
(Matthew 11:28-30, NIV).

Reflection

Self-care is giving the world the best of you, not what is left of you. - Katie Reed

- Have you considered respite care for your family? How would that impact your child(ren)?
- What can you do on a regular basis to rejuvenate yourself and have quality time with your spouse?

Prayer

Dear Lord, I am tired, and grow weary. I cannot care for others well if I do not take care of myself. Please help me lighten my load, practice healthy boundaries, and learn to ask for help when needed. Grant me rest and restore my soul. In Jesus' name, Amen.

40. Simply Prepared

By Julie P. Watson

"For it is by grace you have been saved, through faith—and this is not from yourselves, it is the gift of God—not by works, so that no one can boast. For we are God's handiwork, created in Christ Jesus to do good works, which God prepared in advance for us to do."
(Ephesians 2:8-10, NIV)

Preparation is the key to becoming successful at anything one pursues. This is equally true for parents. Yet, in reality, most parents having biological children are rarely prepared for the arrival of their precious new bundle of joy! No matter how much they prepare, they never really feel ready to become 100% responsible for another living, breathing human being. Or, at least that's what all of my friends and family told me of their own parenting experiences.

Yet, when you go through the rigorous process of becoming a licensed or certified foster parent, preparation is all you do for months on end. From the day we signed up to become foster parents to the day we got our official certification, took nearly six months. Then, we waited another four months before we received our placement. Ten months—that's more waiting time than the nine-month gestation period of a biological child—and that was just to foster! It would be another twenty-one months on top of that before our three children legally joined our family through adoption.

Between training classes about the fostering process, to training on behavioral/emotional/developmental/sexual/educational/social issues the kids may have, to health & safety credentials needed, to continuing education courses required to keep certifications current, to required marriage therapy—what time was left to prepare emotionally, mentally, and spiritually ourselves? Very little—but we did! Next to our decision to marry, our decision to parent was the most important one we'd ever made as a married couple.

One thing that was essential for our preparation was surrounding ourselves with people who could pray for us throughout this incredible journey. Our Bible study home group from our church was instrumental in helping us prepare spiritually. One couple in particular became our mentors. Being older parents of ten grown adults, four of whom were adopted out of foster care, and the husband himself being a foster child—they were (and still are) a blessing straight from heaven! God knew exactly who we needed during this time, and He provided them in spades. In fact, the whole church body embraced our children as our own from day one and loved them like extended family members. Our children always felt very special!

And while I hemmed and hawed at the idea of being "required" to take six sessions of marital counseling—I'm glad we did! Our Christian counselor helped us fine-tune some things in our marriage in preparation, and also things we needed to examine and re-strengthen (i.e. like taking time to spend together and reconnect—this became super important once kids entered our lives). Another valuable preparatory exercise he had us perform during therapy was evaluating our parenting styles (both from our own childhood experiences in how our parents parented us, as well as how we thought we would parent based on various scenarios given). Some interesting things came out of that. The most important was that we needed to be unified as parents. Kids like to divide and conquer if they see even the slightest weakness. Boy, are we glad we paid attention to that session!

Our daughter regularly tried to not only divide us, but literally drive a wedge between my husband and me. She was extremely manipulative in her survival techniques. She had clearly used them before on past foster parents with some success, I imagined. And, since she came to us wanting only a mother, not knowing what it was to have a father in her life, she was detached from my husband from day one. She would lie to each of us while presenting a picture of blame in his corner and approval in mine—she was trying to win me over and secure my loyalty, so to speak. I saw this over and over and tried to lovingly approach her with what she was doing, trying to show her that I understood why, based on what she'd gone through in her young life.

However, after many months of seeing no improvement and realizing she didn't plan on stopping, I finally had enough. I got down on my knees, looked her square in the eye, and got very serious. I told her quite simply, but firmly, "Your dad is my husband, and God made us one when we got married seventeen years ago, which was for life, no matter what. Therefore, what you think you're going to do with this behavior is only going to backfire, actually making everything harder for you. He and I will always be in unity, even if we don't always agree. YOU cannot separate us—EVER—so stop trying!" And with that, she rarely, if ever, tried doing it again. After our adoption we did attachment therapy (which, while very strange to me personally, did help somewhat). "Daddy and Daughter" dances also greatly helped their relationship thrive. Today they're close, but ultimately, she still prefers Mom (at least for now, but teenage years are just a stone's throw away).

Agreeing to be in unity with your spouse is the parenting preparation gift that keeps on giving! Remember, being in unity doesn't mean you'll agree on everything, but it reminds you to discuss matters that arise and to come to the children unified with your final decision (even if it wasn't what you initially wanted). Don't let the kids see a window of opportunity—your unity in marriage is one of your greatest strengths throughout this whole parenting journey.

Reflection

Preparation is very much a Biblical principle. It's repeated as a theme time and again; from Noah preparing the ark for the coming flood, to five virgins with oil in their lamps prepared for the coming bridegroom, examples are not difficult to find. The common theme, however, is that those who are prepared are ultimately saved from coming tribulation(s). As foster/adoptive parents there'll be quite a few trials and tribulations—and they definitely won't be only with the children. But, if you are prepared, have a team of committed people praying you through, and are unified with your spouse, you are going to get through every trial with the Lord's help!

Prayer

Dear Lord, in Your grace and provision, please prepare me in every way I need it—both known and unknown. I ask You to provide committed friends and family to continually surround us in prayer throughout this journey. I pray for Your wisdom and understanding in dealing with everything our child(ren) has (have) already gone through or will go through. Help me to cling to my spouse, and help us to remain unified, regardless of our opinions. We know this will honor You and help our child(ren) see love in action between loving and committed spouses. Thank You, Lord, we know this is Your will, as preparation is a principle repeated in Your Word. We love You! Amen!

41. Simply Reunited

By Tracy Loken Weber

" And we know that in all things God works for the good of those who love him, who have been called according to his purpose." (Romans 8:28, NIV)

Reunification. To us, this was our calling as a couple. To bring a sibling group placed in foster care together again, to provide siblings a stable and loving home forever.

After being licensed we finally received our call to action. The county was looking for a forever placement for a sibling group of three. After almost two years of separation, one of the foster homes was preparing to move to Texas. This was the driving factor for the county to begin the process of reuniting a sibling group of three into our care. At the time it appeared that they would not be reunifying with their biological family and the county was looking for a forever home for this sibling group of three. On our ninth wedding anniversary, the oldest of the three children joined our home. This little boy wearing an orange Star

Wars t-shirt came to live with us and to begin weekly visits with his sisters. He was so excited, yet moved in with scarlet fever. So, for the next few weeks we focused on bonding with him, helping him recover from scarlet fever and making plans to see his beloved sisters.

His sisters remained in their current foster placement for two months, and during that time we had weekly visits, weekend visits, and even a full week of having them all reacclimate to one another and to our home. During this time, the children were inseparable. Our foster son, their brother, had to sit in the middle of the girls. On the sofa, lying on the floor, in the car, outside playing, in the pool, at the dining room table, no matter where they were, he was surrounded by his two sisters. Their love for one another was and still is so powerful to witness. It was evident their natural bond as siblings was powerful and pure. This sense of natural strength they shared as siblings, no matter how much time had passed, was so powerful to witness. It was time for this sibling group to be reunited.

While they were in foster care, before being placed with us, they did have minimal visits. Visits happened every other month for about an hour or so, and an occasional overnight happened, but the visits were limited. Either way, the children were not together on a daily or weekly basis. They missed each other so much! During their time together, we witnessed constant hugs and joyous playtime. They just couldn't wait until their next visit.

From early in the morning hours, until late at night, they were all about reconnecting their bond. We welcomed endless hours of playtime, allowing space for reconnection, for memories and drawing out what they remembered. Even though they were the tender ages of one, three, and four when they were removed from their biological family, they needed that time to just be siblings again, now at the ages of three, five, and six.

When the girls finally moved in, they had holes in their shoes, clothing too small for their growing bodies, and nothing for them to begin school in two days. I quickly went to the store and with the school list in hand, began to shop for our middle foster child to go to kindergarten. She had just turned five and needed everything from a backpack full of school supplies, to two pairs of shoes, to new underwear, tooth brush, clothing, hair brush, and so much more, all of which was not supported financially by anyone but us.

The first few months was definitely the "honeymoon period" of behaviors, and as they became more comfortable in our home, their behaviors slowly became more difficult. As we were allowing time for reconnection and for them to get to know each other again, their healing journey was also in progress. The added stress of getting to know us, having them to be up and ready for another new school, yet to be separated again to attend school and daycare and homework, was all there. We were STRESSED to the max with minimal support from local friends, no family nearby, no respite care, no support period, all while maintaining our two full-time careers. Within two months we went from no children to three, all with severe mental health special needs spanning from anxiety, post-traumatic stress disorder, attention deficit hyperactivity disorder, neglect, to trauma,... and in time more mental health diagnosis were identified.

As they all settled into our home with a new school and routine, they felt safe and secure. That's when the real trauma began to show its ugly head. We began multiple weekly therapies for which we are still very active five years later, and due to the severity of their trauma, this will be a lifelong need for our adopted children.

After the children had been in foster care for over four years, the day that they were waiting for finally came, their adoption day. It was here. The day they knew they were together forever was about to be declared for all to see. Friends and family came in from out-of-state. We arrived at the courthouse, and their pure excitement was something that could not be contained. The honorable judge went through the court proceedings and at the end asked each one of the children to come up to the bench. He stated that this Monday morning at 9 o'clock, adoption was the highlight of his week as he gave the children his gavel to make his order for adoption legal. As one stared up at the judge smiling, another was jumping for joy and clapping her hands, and the third sibling at the tender age of four was banging the gavel, with both of her little hands wrapped around the small wooden handle of the gavel.

After the official proceedings the honorable judge came over and said how powerful our testimonial was about how the children were together all the time once they were reunited. He stated how he needed to do a better job of keeping siblings together and that after my personal testimonial he was doing everything in his power to make sure siblings stayed together while in foster placement and through the adoption process.

The power of keeping sibling groups together for life is one amazing experience to witness. Our home has been blessed beyond measure with sweet moments of praise and thanksgiving from the children for their reunification.

Reflection

- How can you help support siblings being reunified and staying together?
- How can you advocate for sibling groups?
- How can you support a family that has adopted a sibling group?

Prayer

Heavenly Father, thank You for those who are able to open up their homes to keep sibling groups together. Let us all be more mindful when it comes to keeping more children together with their siblings in their forever placements. Use me to keep siblings together and to help out where I'm able. Help me use this time for Your will, and guide my focus to where it needs to be. In Your Son's name I pray, Amen.

42. Simply Rooted

By Tracy Loken Weber

" So then, just as you received Christ Jesus as Lord, continue to live your lives in him, rooted and built up in him, strengthened in the faith as you were taught, and overflowing with thankfulness."
(Colossians 2:6-7, NIV)

Just like the old oak tree, we all have our roots and individual heritage. Deep down we all want to know where we came from; we want to know our story. Now imagine having been uprooted, taken from your family, and placed in foster care. Having to endure moving in and out of multiple foster homes with different heritages, various family cultures and celebrations. The memories of life before foster care becomes blurred. Who am I? Where did I come from? Who do I look like? Many foster children have asked, "Why didn't my parents love me enough to change what they were doing to keep me? Why do I have to be different from all the other kids?"

Tough questions. Grieving their losses is not incompatible with celebrating their triumphs. Yes, this child will teach you more than you will ever teach them. Their resilience and ability to overcome their past will at times overcome you and create in you a new heart full of a deeper compassion. A heart full of this incredible love, hope, and understanding.

At the end of the day, they are children first. They are children who have been handed a difficult start to their lives, their roots have been broken; yet that doesn't define who they are. Remember to never ask, "What's wrong with you?" but ask, "What happened to you?" It's up to you to dig deep for the answers and to advocate for them. Trust your gut and don't be concerned with what others say or do. You know your child the best, and it's okay to say "no" to doctors and therapists. You must advocate for what's best for your child and for your family.

Remember that often the greatest miracles will come in the biggest mess. Welcome the messes, because you never know what may come of it. During this time you will become the army for your child, ready for battle at a moment's notice. Ready to do what's right, ready and armed to meet their individual needs. Ready to educate others to know how to best serve your child. This alone will lead you to become an educator, trainer, specialist, therapist, counselor, negotiator, advocate, peacemaker, and a "silo-breaker-downer."

Believe it or not, you are now part of a secret, hidden world that everyone is either afraid of or ashamed to talk about. A world that will open your eyes to things you never imagined before. You will witness experts in the field making forever judgments on your child. You will see firsthand racism, discrimination, rudeness, evil glares, ignorance, educational systems lacking trauma-informed classrooms and support, silos of broken systems, lack of mental health services, mental health hospitals not equipped with enough rooms to help your child, a waiting list for another waiting list that you have been waiting on for almost a year, yet to find out that you must continue to wait more to receive help.

Your number finally comes up. That waiting list of nine months, it's finally your time. Yet the help comes nine months too late, six mental health hospitalizations too late. You are exhausted from the daily battles, the constant living in "fight or flight" mode. When the help finally arrives, it does so with more paperwork to complete, more interviews to take place, more people now learning more about your family. More home visits, workers coming and going, yet again training new workers as they take over your case. New faces once again coming into your child's life. A new person now making the calls on what supports your family does and does not receive. The silos of help are in systems that are overloaded with so many needs, never enough staff to meet the demands. You become overloaded advocating for your child's needs, your family needs help, the trauma continues, they regress, the roots continue to grow in different directions.

Beneath the surface of the changing seasons of our lives, something is taking root. Due to complex systems in play, healing takes longer. Something deep within us and our child is stirring, healing, and causing the pain of the past to slowly fade away. Our roots begin to grow in a different direction, this time rooted in healing and forgiveness. You will witness so many little everyday miracles, and you will smile seeing these little changes come, knowing you are witnessing a life change for the better. These children's walls will slowly come down. Their creativity will begin to shine through. Their giggles and smiles will lighten the daily load of healing. You will find ways to stay motivated to press on and connect with others who are also thrusted into this secret hidden world helping others to find their voice. You will stay rooted deeply in compassion and love for others and in hope for the future.

Love and Hope. Deeply rooted in love and hope for all the brighter days ahead.

Reflection

- How can you help support stability for my child?
- How can you advocate for this child? What efforts do I need to change and say "no" to?
- How can you share this "hidden world" with others through advocacy and educational efforts?

Prayer

Heavenly Father, I pray for change. I pray for the silos to be broken. I pray for complex systems to come together, to work together, and to truly communicate to meet the needs of so many children crying out for help. Let us all be more mindful when it comes to navigating complex systems and helping these precious child(ren) in our care. Help me use this time for Your will, and guide my focus to where it needs to be. In Your Son's name I pray, Amen.

43. Simply Sad

By Julie P. Watson

"Religion that God our Father accepts as pure and faultless is this: to look after orphans and widows in their distress and to keep oneself from being polluted by the world."
(James 1:27 , NIV)

If you are currently a foster parent, or even considering becoming one, you likely came to this decision after hearing some rather startling and heart-wrenching statistics. The foster care system is overburdened. Estimates range from 400,000 to 500,000 foster children currently in the system and not appearing to lighten up anytime soon. This is far too many, but it's the reality in which we live. So, what do we do?

If you're a Christian, and likely you are if you picked up this devotional, then you're probably here because you feel called to care for children in difficult parental circumstances. Notice I didn't say orphans. Yes, God calls us to care for orphans and widows as stated in James 1:27. However, we must acknowledge that most children in foster care HAVE parents. Very few are literal orphans (children whose parents have died). However, for one reason or another these kids' parents have lost them either temporarily or permanently due to substance abuse, criminal behavior, neglect, endangerment, abuse (all kinds), and, yes, death of the parents with no living relative either available or able to care for them. But, in reading the whole verse in James, we see that it identifies those who are "in their distress," and these kids certainly fit that description.

The big picture here is that children love their parents (yes, even those being abused) and want to be with them. So, to take on the role of foster parent to a child who doesn't necessarily want you, is a VERY difficult calling, indeed. I know a lot of people have really negative feelings toward foster care, and many believe foster care parents are only in it for a "paycheck." That, sadly, may be true for some. But, from my experience, and the many foster parents I've personally met, I believe the majority are truly doing it as a calling in their life to help a child and his or her parents reunite! Reunification is always the goal for foster care IF the biological parent(s) are willing to do all the court requires to get their child(ren) back.

Sadly, that doesn't always happen, as was the case with my children. My eldest son spent one month shy of five years in foster care, and his half-siblings spent just over four years in foster care. The parental rights were terminated after eighteen months for the two youngest, because whatever was required by the court wasn't completed. My older son had more time because a maternal grandmother took him in for the first nine months. This ended up being a disaster, as she was mentally ill, and he was eventually removed from her care. He rejoined his siblings after all that time with much disruption in that foster home.

It still breaks my heart what they went through without each other for so long.

Long story short, we went into foster care with a desire to adopt siblings who were just sitting in the system with no way out because parental rights were already terminated. It broke our hearts to think of so many children never getting the opportunity to be a part of a loving family after what they had already lost. We heard those same, sad statistics you heard about children a certain age not getting adopted. We were ready for older children, pre-teens, and even teens, so often forgotten and shuffled around from home to home, or even worse, placed into group homes. We wanted to do what we could to prevent that and give them a permanent, loving home and family.

What we weren't prepared for was the system itself. The county we fostered/adopted from is one of the most crowded and busy in our state. It's also one of the poorest as well as one with the highest drug use/abuse. In the twenty-one months we fostered, we went through a total of ten different social workers and learned a great deal about that specific county. Two different social workers told us that every social worker in their county had over one hundred cases each. That fact alone blew us away! There aren't enough hours in a day or month to properly check on one hundred different cases each month. For comparison, social workers in our residing county average thirty to forty cases each.

I remember our very first "check-in" with the kids' social worker. First, I offered to drive to a half-way point since the drive was so long from her county to ours. Our meeting lasted less than five minutes. We met in a Walmart parking lot. She got out of her car, looked in ours at these three little kids who were so excited to see her after being apart for nearly a month, and all she said was, "Hi, looks like you're all doing great!" She asked me two or three questions about how they were handling the transition and whether they had started school yet. That was the gist of it, and then she was gone. The kids were so disappointed! She had been their one constant for the previous two and a half years—they each had things they wanted to tell her themselves.

However, this is the reality of an overtaxed county child welfare department. We were told other things, which were quite disturbing. Because we cannot verify them, I will not share them, but one thing was for sure—there was very little work being done on our children's case! Sadly, we found out about a year after we started fostering (and going round and round with several social workers), that the kids' original social worker had gotten sick about four or five months beforehand and had taken a leave of absence. She apparently died sometime during that time frame (to this day, I still don't know when), but no one ever told us—I had to ask what happened to her. My children cried over her passing, especially not being able to say goodbye. It was a difficult experience in more ways than one.

None of it was a surprise to the Lord—He is well aware of the dire straits every child is going through in foster care. He knows the challenges we'll face before we are even certified. But, trusting Him to finish a good work within us has to be our prayer request from the beginning. There may be many times along the journey you feel like giving up, but hold fast—the Lord will strengthen you to finish the race. It's an important one, and these children are depending on you to help them through it. Just be willing to recommit when you want to quit. God will take care of the rest!

Reflection

God is in the midst of every circumstance, especially regarding children. They are important to Him and it hurts His heart when they suffer. Remember, these horrible circumstances are the result of a sinful world—God didn't cause them. He allows bad things to happen since He knows we will draw near to Him in order to heal and persevere. This will, in turn, deepen our relationship with Him and help us grow in our faith. The difficult thing is explaining this to the children in your care. However, it's possible. Don't forget that we are all called to overcome—this includes our children! He has a divine purpose and plan for each of us, but to fulfill it, we must overcome the obstacles in our lives that will strengthen us for that exact journey ahead!

Prayer

Dear Lord, please be with each and every child in the foster care system. Comfort their hearts, as they are missing their parents, no matter the circumstances. Help me to be compassionate and loving to their needs, wants, and hurts. I want to finish all that You called me to do. Lead me in Your will, desire, and chosen plan for each child in my care. I love You, Lord. I wish to serve You by loving these children who may not know You or Your love. Help me show them who You are by my words, but especially by my actions. Thank You, Jesus! Amen.

44. Simply Scared

By Julie P. Watson

"Be strong and courageous. Do not be afraid or terrified because of them, for the Lord your God goes with you; he will never leave you nor forsake you."
(Deuteronomy 31:6 , NIV)

Few things in life can scare you to your very core. Oh sure, there are phobias such as snakes, spiders, heights, flying, and being confined in small spaces. But, have you ever considered things that shake your inner-self so hard you're not sure if, let alone when, you'll ever be able to breathe normally again? For example, a freak accident where you barely escape death? Or, how about losing your small child in a large crowd for even just a minute or two? Would these send shockwaves of fear throughout your entire being, right down to your fingertips? Why do they cause so much more fear than the aforementioned phobias? Quite simply—they have potential for great loss.

Now, picture yourself as a small child, say four or five years old. In a breathless moment you're being yanked from your home, taken by police officers and other unfamiliar adults, separated from your parents, your bed, your toys, your clothes, your pets, your friends, your school... your everything. You have no idea what's happening, nor when or if you'll ever see those things again. You've just lost your entire known world and entered foster care. Welcome!

If you're one of the lucky ones, you might have been able to grab some clothing and maybe even a toy or two, all thrown into a black trash bag for easy transport. Your belongings, or what's left of everything you own in this world, now resemble a big bag of garbage. You're introduced to adult after adult until your assigned case worker takes you to some place called a "foster home" where you're presented to a foster mom, and possibly a foster dad, who become your "temporary" guardians. There might even be other foster kids there, of which, you're now one. And, if all the stars are in alignment and fate smiles upon your face, you might even have your siblings join you in this very same foster home.

Get the picture? This all-too-familiar occurrence is earth-shattering to these children. Yes, even to those being horribly abused! The familiar, even painful familiar, is far more reassuring than the unknown. Fear is the only thing they will be certain of having within the first few days, to weeks, to months, in foster care. Sadly, some kids carry the fears and trauma into their lives for years afterwards, never to find healing.

The fight-or-flight mechanism for survival kicks in from day one. It's something we all have. We are wired to either stay and fight the entity that's causing us fear or run and hide from it. Depending on how long children are in the system, they can stay in fight-or-flight survival mode for years, often making it difficult to transition once out of the system. Adoptive parents are taught that for every year a child is in foster care, it takes two years of stability in a post-adoptive world to normalize, if at all. The statistics themselves are scary, but God is in the midst, helping us through this journey.

All three of our kids had fears of some kind. My eldest son was the most emotional and fearful. For the first six months, noises, lights, and shadows outside his window at night would get him worked up into nightly crying fits. He would also have nightmares and talk, yell, or cry out in fear during his sleep, often not remembering anything upon waking. He often relived bad memories and would wake more tired than before he went to sleep (this went on for over two years). He was easily startled by everything, and I wondered how I was going to help him through all his past traumas, scary memories, and many disappointments. God knew.

We began singing songs, starting with "Jesus Loves Me," and prayed together every single night, then worked up to reading and memorizing Scripture. The verse 2 Timothy 1:7 became our nightly verse, "For God has not given us a spirit of fear, but of power and of love and of a sound mind." My son has an amazing memory, and reciting verses and singing songs to himself was how he learned to self-soothe so he could return to sleep without waking us. I'm so happy to say, he is a much happier, stronger, more confident child today with few fears. He loves the Lord and knows more Scripture than most adults!

My daughter's greatest fear was that I would not return whenever I left the house. She would often act out to get negative attention or melt down into an uncontrollable crying fit. Her fears stemmed from regular bouts of neglect when her biological mother would take off for days at a time, leaving her with another person in the house. After a year and a half of seeing this fearful behavior, and never giving her reason to fear my not coming home, I finally got down on my knees, looked her in the eye and said, "Honey, have I ever not come home, even once before?"

She tearfully answered, "No."

I continued, "Haven't I proved to you by now that I'm not like your bio mom?"

"Yes," she said.

"Then I'm going to tell you right here and now, you NEVER have to fear this, because I ALWAYS come home to my family, and you're my family!" And, with that, she never repeated her behavior. It was the breakthrough I had prayed for! She needed to alter her beliefs based on observed facts, not bad memories. Her definition of a mother was changing from one who left and didn't return for days, to one who left but always returned the same day. With God's help, I was able to show her through repeated, reliable actions that my word was true and she could trust me.

My youngest son wasn't too fearful himself (mainly new people and loud sounds), but he was more reactive to his brother's fears. Since they share a room, it was hard to separate them. We actually did separate them for about seven months, but my oldest son became destructive. He was afraid of being alone, even in his own room. So, back to the shared room he went, and we dealt with their fears jointly. My youngest son was also unable to cope properly; his biggest issue was social withdrawal. He would hide behind furniture so he wouldn't have to deal with any negative stimuli. Singing, praying, and reciting verses also helped him with his issues (along with improving his slight speech delay). He was our "easy" kid. Since he's a bit of a comedian and LOVES to be tickled, laughter brought healing relief.

So, as you can see, God gives you all the tools you need for each child in your care. No matter the fear, everything can be overcome with time, love, patience, understanding, reassurance, and some godly deposits in their life. After all, "if God is for us, who can be against us?" (Romans 8:31). "No weapon formed against [us] shall prosper" (Isaiah 54:17a). Feed these truths into your little ones' hearts and minds, and fear won't be able to keep a grip on them!

Reflection

God knows all the fears your child(ren) have, and He wants to help you combat those fears for life. This requires daily communication with the Lord in prayer, song, and Scripture, for them and you. Teach them by modeling a robust spiritual life and regular connection with the Heavenly Father. Use examples from Scripture to teach your child(ren) how those in the Bible overcame fear: Esther is a favorite in our home. Even if some of your child(ren)'s fears are a surprise to you, none are a surprise to God. Reach out to Him—He's ready to heal all the fears within your home's walls, including your own.

Prayer

Dear Lord, help me to look to You when I am afraid. Modeling this behavior will show my child(ren) where to look when they are afraid. Help me guide them toward you in all things, but especially to understand that fear is a liar; You are Truth who gives perfect peace! Father, help me to be patient and show them compassion in all they're going through, even things that seem small or don't make sense. You know where these fears come from, and only You can quiet their hearts and minds, allowing them to heal from the inside out. I love how You always know just how to help me to help them. Thank You, Lord! Amen

45. Simply Showing Love

By Amy

Somebody once commented that when she gave birth to her daughter, she loved her as soon as she saw her, but it must be different when you adopt a child. The first time our children visited our home, we walked to the park together. As we walked home we passed a house with rocks around the mailbox. Our daughter, age four, sat down and started throwing the rocks into the street. I asked her to stop, and she looked right at me and kept throwing them. That act of defiance was just a taste of what was to come.

It's hard to show love when you're constantly fighting battles. And yes, it's hard to show love when you're focused on the outbursts, yelling, and hurt. One of my favorite verses is Romans 5:8, "But God shows His love for us in that while we were still sinners, Christ died for us" (ESV). I was, and still am, in rebellion towards God. While I was sinning, before I even repented and asked for forgiveness, He died for me. Amazing! God calls me to sacrificial love, even during the hurt. Love isn't given because it is earned; it's given because love is from God (1 John 4:7).

We recently planted some grass seed in the corner of our yard. We try to water several times a day, but the ground still dries out. It should be showing signs of life, but the seed is just lying there, dormant, and I'm a little worried that it's not going to grow. Am I watering my children's hearts? Even though I may not see any change in the midst of the struggle, I have to believe that God is mending their hearts. I can't make seed sprout and take root, only God can. It is my job to water and tend, and trust that God will do what I cannot.

During summer break, I loved the peaceful, quiet moments in the morning while my children were still sleeping. I didn't look forward to the seemingly endless days which would inevitably include fights among siblings and conflict between parent and child. I love the quote from Toni Morrison, "Your eyes should light up when your child enters the room." She went on to say, "We adults often feel let down when children don't make the progress we wish they would. This eventually affects the relationship between the child and parent or teacher. After enough negative interactions, whenever the child and adult walk into a room and see each other their eyes roll in grief. How many of our students go from class to class, from teacher to teacher, consistently getting disapproval? Wouldn't it make a huge difference in the lives of these students if instead of getting disapproval, they saw our eyes light up? 'Johnny, you're here! I was hoping you would make it today!'"

Reflection

- How can you show sacrificial love to your children, even in the midst of their rebellion?

Prayer

Heavenly Father, thank You for loving me unconditionally. Thank You for sending Your Son to die for me while I was still sinning. Please help me to show Your unconditional love to the children You have entrusted to me for this short time. Help me to show them that no matter what they do, they are loved. May they see and feel Your love through me. Amen

46. Simply Siblings

By Brenda & Steve Wagenknecht

" As he looked about and saw his brother Benjamin, his own mother's son, he asked, "Is this your youngest brother, the one you told me about?" And he said, "God be gracious to you, my son." Deeply moved at the sight of his brother, Joseph hurried out and looked for a place to weep. He went into his private room and wept there. After he had washed his face, he came out and, controlling himself, said, "Serve the food."
(Genesis 43:29-31, NIV)

Joseph and his brothers were siblings with a history. His brothers knew Joseph was favored by their father. The jealousy led the brothers to do the unthinkable—sell him into slavery after attempting to kill him, then lie to their father saying Joseph was dead. Betrayal and years of separation led to an unimaginable family rift. Their father kept praying for his children. A miracle brought the siblings back together. A miracle that was based on forgiveness that only is known only through Jesus' death for our forgiveness.

A sibling is defined as a brother or a sister, sharing a parent. When God brings families together through foster care and adoption, He makes new siblings. They grow, learn, and develop under the guidance of the same parents. They experience the same culture of food, communication, values, dress, habits, etc. These experiences develop bonds that go beyond blood and genetics—they create siblings.

Early on in motherhood, I realized my children were going to teach me much more than I could ever teach them about life. Looking back, there were little moments of parenting that made a profound impact. Moments that stopped me in my tracks, now frozen in time, are so deeply ingrained into my memory that I see the life-changing experiences as clearly as if they happened yesterday. Moments that were so profound; yet, so simple. Experiencing the unconditional love between siblings became one of the first of these life lessons moments.

I unexpectedly learned one lesson as the sun rose on the first morning after we brought our daughter home. On that cold and dark January morning in Idaho, less than a year after moving back to the States after three years in the warm Carribean, we were still adjusting and acclimating to what winter was. Our pudgy-cheeked three-year-old excitedly climbed into our bed, his face grinning with pure joy! He was our 6:00 am wake-up call every morning. He would usually wake me up to tell me it was time to organize his daily schedule of magnetic pictures on the refrigerator door. The structure and routine helped him feel safe and calm after the stress of moving. (Another thing my children taught me early on!)

This morning was different, though. He climbed into bed with my husband and me because he knew I had returned home late the evening before with his baby sister. His cold hands and feet crawled up and over me until he found her. The dimpled, beaming smile on his face is etched in my memory. He looked at me. Then he looked at the burrito-wrapped bundle. He looked at my husband. Then he looked again at his sister's hands peeking out of the footprint-patterned hospital blanket.

"Mom, is this my new sister? Can I see her?" Andrew asked with such great electrical energy that it seemed to radiate out of every pore of his body. I smiled and assured him that his sister was finally home. He ever so gently pulled back the blankets as his eyes widened to a size I don't think I had ever seen. His smile grew larger with every inch of the blanket he pulled back. When he had a full view of his baby sister, his simple response revealed just how welcome she would be in our family. Gently caressing her dimpled cheeks, he exclaimed, "Oh, mommy! She is black! She is SO beautiful!"

"Yes! She is black! Yes! She is so beautiful!" I responded as I watched a miracle: an immediate and an unconditional love blossom between two children who had no biological connection, yet, were fully siblings. Andrew leaned over and kissed his baby sister's forehead. I knew that he would always be her protector. I had seen this miracle twice before when we brought our other children home, but it still took my breath away.

Throughout childhood these children were typical siblings—they laughed together, they built forts together, they transformed toy box lids into boats to slide down the steps together, they secretly watched shows that I thought they were too young for, and yes, they had moments of "not liking each other." However, as my children also taught me, the difficult times created opportunities to apologize and offer forgiveness. These situations built the bonds between siblings that will be the glue that connects them for a lifetime.

Homeschooling siblings together gave our family opportunities to spend time together building memories. I was a public school teacher and had never imagined I would homeschool, but sometimes God just abruptly puts you where He needs you. I doubted our homeschooling path for years. Looking back now after graduating two sons from homeschooling, I realize how many blessings flowed from it—family time, shared experiences, learning together as a cohort, learning from and with siblings with special needs, and so many more. All these interactions built connections and shaped them into siblings that can rely on each other into adulthood.

That little three-year-old Andrew who immediately adored his new sister, grew into a protective older brother, as we expected. He built forts for his younger siblings, watched over his younger brother with autism, and sat by his sister's bedside when she was ill. That newborn girl grew into a bold personality who drug her brothers on new and exciting adventures. She is not afraid to say difficult truths to keep her siblings in line.

As with any family, we experienced challenges raising five very diverse children. Our five blessings represent five different nationalities, with five unique biological family backgrounds, and multiple special needs. All of them joined our family at varied ages from birth to sixteen. As parents, we have had many sleepless nights worrying about our children's health, education, faith, and future. We pray daily for our children's relationships with each other. As siblings, there have been times of disagreement, hurt feelings, and embarrassment. As with all families, individual siblings often voice differing perspectives of the same experiences. Times of poor communication have led to misunderstandings. There has been a temptation to let these challenges cause a distancing between siblings. Yet, in the end, our family is our safety net—a secure place to fall no matter what life brings. As parents, we pray that we have taught our children to trust each other when we need help, when we need advice, when we need a shoulder to help bear our burdens, and when we share each other's joys. While our skin tones may be as varied as the colors in Joseph's coat of many colors, we are family, and siblings are simply siblings.

Reflection

Our family is our safety net—a secure place to fall no matter what life brings.

How can you foster the sibling bond between my children and build positive relationships?

Prayer

Heavenly Father, thank You for bringing families together through a variety of ways and in Your perfect timing. Strengthen the bonds between siblings so that they may experience the blessings of companionship and unconditional love. Guard our hearts to trust that You work things for the good of Your children, even those difficult and messy family situations. Forgive us when we take our parents and siblings for granted. Amen.

47. Simply Snowed in with a Child-Like Faith

By Tracy Loken Weber

" We were therefore buried with him through baptism into death in order that, just as Christ was raised from the dead through the glory of the Father, we too may live a new life."
(Romans 6:4, NIV)

Overnight a snowstorm leaving twelve inches of heavy, wet snow found us the next morning snowed-in and preparing for home church. Our seven-year-old foster child at the time, stepped up to lead our praise, arranging the entire service, even writing a poem. She read from her Bible where little Post-it notes flagged different verses. We even sang a few songs from the hymnal. Then she began to read her poem that she wrote in about five minutes. She poured her little heart out as my husband and I began to cry. Immediately our faith and spirit were renewed; God was present. Her poem became lyrics that were turned into a song for her holy baptism a few short months later. On the very same day she was adopted with her siblings, all three children were baptized, and we were blessed to have her song sung at the baptism and adoption celebration with our dear friends and family. The song "We Praise You, Holy God" has been professionally recorded and is being sung across the nation.

We Praise You Holy God

Lyrics by Samiyrah Weber; Music by Wendysue Fluegge - May, 2017

Sun shining in my heart from Jesus Christ my God

He shines from heaven - Glory be to God!

His soul is golden bright

Those who believe will see His light

He is forgiveness - Glory be to God!

We praise you We praise you Oh, we praise You, Holy God!

We praise you We praise you Oh, we praise you, Holy God!

My soul white I am baptized Jesus in my heart -

I am His child Oh, Glory be to God!

With His Holiness He has saved us from our sins -

The One I love - yea, Glory be to God!

We praise you We praise you Oh, we praise you Holy God!

We praise you We praise you Oh, we praise you Holy God!

Wow. Those poetic words, these lyrics from a seven-year-old. Yes! God was moving through her, His message, and she was the vessel.

What was once a simple Sunday morning at home became a spiritual renewal by a precious child of God at the tender age of seven. We all live very busy lives. Allow for your family to slow down. Just as our daughter is healing from her traumatic past, her love for Jesus shines through her every day. Her lyrics are moving others, transforming lives, and renewing a child-like faith in us all. What a blessing those twelves inches of snow was for our family. Our lives were forever changed as we embraced the unexpected quiet time at home worshipping our Lord and Savior.

Reflection

- What do you need to do to slow down our family?
- What positives can you share about my child? What are they good at? How do they thrive?
- How can we create more time at home to be with God?

Prayer

Heavenly Father, when nature throws our family a curveball, let us respond with calm and intention. Allow us to create space to hear You and to allow our children to lead us. In Your Son's name I pray, Amen.

48. Simply Teamwork

By Brenda Wagenknecht

It was Super Bowl Sunday. Our three elementary-aged kiddos had friends over. They were making a lot of noise in Nerf gun battles throughout the house with short spurts of cheering when catching a glimpse of a big play in the Big Game. I nearly missed the cell phone when it rang in the other room. My husband answered it and walked away to escape the intense noise. Soon he returned with a puzzled look on his face. He motioned for me to join him in a quiet room where we could both hear the phone on speaker. The question from our friend, a fellow pastor, on the other end took some time to process. Could we help?

An adoptive family was in need. Their son, whom they loved, had many special needs. He suffered from the effects of bathing in drugs and alcohol in utero for nine months. After birth he suffered the trauma of being removed from his birth mother. The withdrawal from the drugs in his system was followed by an autism diagnosis at the age of three. Now, he was nearly six years old, nonverbal, still wearing diapers. Their son's special needs isolated the family, and the therapy and doctor appointments overwhelmed them beyond their coping capacity. They simply did not know how to care for their son. They could not do many things as a family because he needed one-on-one care. The parents were exhausted from years of intense caregiving. They needed help. They needed respite. They needed a team to take the baton for the next leg of the race—the next years of raising the boy whom they loved.

Our friend thought my husband and I were an obvious choice to call. We had fostered and adopted, and we knew there may be more children that God would bring into our lives whether it would be short-term or long-term. Our previous adoption journeys had been as unique as the individuality of each of our children. Our previous situations had familiarized us with the "teamwork" of fostering and adopting that resulted in our children joining our family. Like many families, Steve and I had spoken of adoption early on in our marriage even before we were blessed with a biological son. However, the discussion became serious when my pregnancy and delivery were riddled with health complications. At this point in life, we could have never imagined the "teamwork" that would be orchestrated to intertwine the families of our future children.

Living overseas made our initial exploration of adoption options very limited. In the meantime, God brought a local Puerto Rican family into our lives. The three teenage sisters had already been separated in different foster homes, but suddenly a change in placement was needed. Social Services had made the decision to reunite the sisters and send them to a boarding school across the island. We became the landing place and newest member of the "team" for the sisters when they came home on weekends and holidays. Eventually, the challenges of living away at boarding school, without the loving care of a family, became too much. Social Services realized they needed to adjust the placement. Our new role on the team became a permanent foster placement for one of the siblings. Never forgetting the rest of her team, we welcomed our daughter with joy!

Then, when we had a two-year-old biological son and a sixteen-year-old foster daughter at home, God brought another family into our lives. A young mom was unable to care for her one-year-old son in the manner she believed he deserved. This young mom loved her son so much that she selflessly used an adoption agency to find a team member to take the baton in caring for her son because she could not provide for his needs. With joy, we joined the team to permanently care for our newest child. We would never forget the difficult decision his birth mother had so lovingly made.

Not long after, another young mom reached out to us through the same adoption agency. She was looking for a family to take the baton for her. A loss of a job, burnt down apartment complex, broken down car, and family unwilling to extend a helping hand led her to us. Her two young daughters were in our care for thirty-six hours—the time the state of Florida gives birth parents to change their minds after legally passing the baton to another family. During those thirty-six hours, we fed, clothed, baptized, and loved Sarah and Tiffany while providing counsel to their mom at the same time. She truly loved her girls and was determined to do what was best for them. When her family came around and offered her assistance, she was unsure what to do. Our job on that particular team meant encouraging her to continue caring for her daughters. We were only needed for a short time, exactly thirty-six hours, but our role was a vital and ultimately life-changing component in the decision this young mother made in the best interests of her two daughters. With joy, we were part of that team that helped a family stay together.

Within a month, we received another call from the same adoption agency. A two-week-old infant girl was in the care of a temporary foster family. A little one who had already experienced the loss of her family needed someone to take the baton. With joy, we joined the team, never meeting a very important member: her birth mother.

When we received the "Super Bowl Sunday" call to join the life relay team for another family who needed help, this background enabled us to enter the situation with the knowledge that God uses people to play important roles in others' lives in foster and adoption. Sometimes the role is short-lived. Sometimes it is a permanent role. Sometimes we disagree with the role God assigns us. Sometimes team members work closely together for life. Sometimes the team members will pass the baton. When we join the caregiving team motivated by God's love and prayerfully seeking to do what is best for children, it will always be a blessing!

God calls each of us to carry out acts of service during our earthly journey. God planned them for us even before we were born. Ephesians 2:10 NIV, "For we are God's handiwork, created in Christ Jesus to do good works, which God prepared in advance for us to do." Working with children, our all-knowing and gracious God has us team up with others. There are many needs, and different people function on family teams. We are called to work together as a team in caring for God's children, whether fostering, adopting, or simply being a loving adult. Sometimes that means a child may enter our home or life for a short time.

Reflection

Joining a care-giving team out of love for God and our children will be a blessing!

- How can you always remember the importance of your children's team members?
- How will you express gratitude to your child-raising teammates?

Prayer

Dear Lord, Please comfort the hearts of Your servants whom You have called to be part of a team, working to raise Your children. May they know that You have chosen the time and duties for them to carry out. You bless their work. You put teams in place to care for Your precious children, and they are a critical part of that team. Give them confidence in their team membership. Comfort them with the knowledge of our Savior Jesus' death and resurrection, knowing that the team will have a blessed reunion in heaven some day! Amen.

49. Simply Therapy

By Tracy Loken Weber

" You are my refuge and my shield; I have put my hope in your word."
(Psalm 119:114, NIV)

At some point in our lives, we all need help. We may turn to close friends, a church member, our pastor, or even a therapist. As a special needs parent, we have needed to extend our reach and scope for supportive services. We have sought out intensive tutoring, homework help, home therapy, and even specialized services. I can honestly say, most children in foster care need a little extra tender loving care and parents who are willing to go the extra mile to advocate endlessly for their needs.

As such, one of our children needed occupational therapy to help with day-to-day tasks like opening up a bottle; tying shoes; fastening snaps; and cognitive, sensory, social, and tactile functions. In addition, she needed further help with following directions, verbalizing her needs,

Simply Dedicated

and making transitions. All are vital life skills for our daughter to learn. After months of patiently waiting for approval and waiting to get in to see an occupational therapist, we found a great one. We faithfully attended weekly therapy for three months for a total of twelve sessions that the insurance approved. At the end of our twelfth session, a huge issue at school erupted that led to the police being called, multiple school members doing a physical hold on our daughter for a long period of time (well over an hour), and a threat to call a Chapter 51 (involuntary commitment for treatment) on her and take this little six-year-old girl away in handcuffs. I was calling all the mental hospitals to find out if there was room, but all three were full, and the only way she would be admitted would be if she was to arrive via ambulance. Thankfully, the local police department worked with us, understood her trauma background, and listened. She was able to calm down with us, her parents. Her father gathered her favorite stuffed animal, tea party set, and her blanket from home and created a little tea party in the middle of the large gym— the gym she had been running around in for over an hour, tearing everything off the walls. After the police left the gym, she began to feel safe again, and, in time, she came over to Dad, sat down for a little safe tea party, took her meds, hugged her stuffed animal, and became stable, yet hyper alert to all that was going on around her.

About a month later as her mental state continued to deteriorate, after three weeks of daily phone calls to have her accepted for the pre-admittance to the mental hospital, in which every day of those three weeks the on-call doctors said that she should be admitted, but, there were no beds available -- we finally received a call that there was a room for her to go back to inpatient care. This time, she was admitted, and I was going to make sure that the doctors had it right this time; she needed to be stabilized. Our family needed for her to be stabilized. We could not continue to live this way anymore.

She was in the hospital for a full month. Upon her release this time, after four other inpatient and neuropsychic exams, all stating that she was needing an IEP, the local school district, after initially denying her an IEP, finally agreed that our daughter does need one.. Ironically after working with the district for 1.5 years, she qualified not only in one area, but in two different IEP categories. However, at this same meeting, it was determined that the school district can no longer meet her learning needs and she would be transitioning to a behavioral school, not a trauma school, with a staff that had little-to-no trauma training. Later to find out, no trauma training at all.

I thought to myself, So here we go: Transitioning to another school for children who struggle with behaviors, no trauma training, no occupational therapy in place, and a new home therapist beginning, due to the previous therapists' insurance approval running out.

Another referral to get occupational therapy going again for our daughter to attend weekly sessions—to find out that our occupational therapist, who our daughter has a good rapport with, was expecting a baby. The therapist shared that due to her pending FMLA leave she recommended only two sessions over two months. This was a drastic reduction, as we had been going every week for twelve weeks. Yet again, another person's needs were being put before the recommendations of doctors and our daughter's needs. The patient, our daughter, was now seven years old and struggling with day-to-day tasks. The home therapist, the county team, and the psychiatrist were completely taken aback by all of this. All believed that weekly occupational therapy would be in the best interest for our daughter. I

Simply Dedicated

requested another referral for the process to begin all over again. Another eight weeks of waiting for approval from the insurance.

One day, the third referral was in motion. After 45 minutes on the phone with central scheduling, I was transferred to another number and got absolutely nowhere for our daughter. Another dead end with recommendations for four other phone numbers to try. Yet again, another wasted day, another day without healing, another day living in and with trauma going unsupported.

The time, energy, and endless phone calls and wasted time in professional systems is so difficult to manage. To have the children entertained and basic needs met so these calls can be made, to make sure the right person is on the other end who is knowledgeable and can make the right intake appointment is key. It's almost like the divine intervention where all the stars, players, and prayers, are perfectly aligned for one simple appointment to be made.

After two hours and forty-eight minutes, success! The blessing in all of this is I finally was able to make an intake appointment for two months from then to begin the process of getting the insurance to authorize her weekly sessions, which would probably be the normal twelve sessions that would take the insurance company four to eight weeks to approve. So, in reality, three-to-four months from now we will finally begin to receive occupational therapy help again.

I continue to be amazed with how many phone calls I make on a weekly basis; how many messages are left as I wait to be called back. Yet all of the daily needs go on. Assignments from school remain the same with no mental health allowances or real understanding. The normal daily routines all remain in place, meals planning, going through school folders, responding to teachers' emails, going to doctor appointments, going to therapy appointments, making future appointments, refilling medications, dealing with daily trauma memories and healing, and so much more. It's exhausting work, and until you really live it, no one really understands the daily pressures and stress. I wonder what life would be like if we all took mental health a little more seriously, if insurances would allow services until the needs are met.

We must do better for our children. We must advocate for mental health. Their little lives depend on our advocacy, support, voice, and mental health needs. We are all change agents.

Reflection

- How can you be more patient?
- What do you need to do to help make changes so other families do not have to endure what you are going through?

Prayer:

Heavenly Father, show me the way. Be the light during the dark times. Help me be patient, loving, and understanding. Guide my thoughts, words, and actions during times of tribulation. Shower me with grace, love, and understanding so I may be at my very best during these times. Give me the patience so see my children through their healing. In Your Son's name I pray, Amen.

50. Simply Ticking

By Tracy Loken Weber

Sustain me, my God, according to your promise, and I will live; do not let my hopes be dashed.

(Psalm 119:116, NIV)

Wait for it. Wait for it.

In the peace, it comes. The ticking sound from the clock on the wall. Is the moment now? Or in five minutes? Maybe an hour? Or, maybe not even today?

And just like that, in a flash before my eyes a fist comes to my face, and my glasses are knocked clear across the room. The rage, the ticking time bomb, has exploded. The nails begin clawing at my neck, my arms; she's biting me as fast as I can try to hold her in a safe hold to protect myself and others around us. The screaming, yelling, and swearing from my baby girl. A raging bull is right here, right now in front of me, attacking me. She honestly sees the previous "moms" who abused her;

she's back in time in a full-on post-traumatic stress disorder (PTSD) manic episode.

How long will this manic PTSD episode last? Thirty minutes or three hours?

In the midst of this chaos, an inner calm takes over. A cooling sensation takes over my entire body. I fully believe that through this horrible valley, God is right there by my side, saying, "Lean on Me, for I am with you." It's these moments that a calmness takes over, I'm able to take my little girl to a safe room and allow for her to process this horrible trauma. I try to hold her and simply say in the calmest voice ever, "You are safe. Come back to me. What happened to you? When you are ready, I am here to listen." I lean in. I wait. I listen.

Then I stop. I listen as the raging continues and repeat those words ever so softly again, and wait…

In time, she deescalates. She's remorseful as she comes back, and often there are no reasons as to what triggered her. She wants to cuddle and be near me. She climbs into my lap. Lays her head on my heart as I ever so gently rub her back.

She's back. She's back from where the trauma runs so deep.

She looks up at me. "Mama, you're the mama that never hurts me. I love you, Mama."

I begin to sing to her; she settles down. The calm returns; I can hear the clock ticking, until the next trauma memory and episode rears its ugly head.

Reflection

- How can you mentally and physically prepare for the explosions to come?
- How can you be more alert to the needs of my child?
- How can you be more present?

Prayer

Heavenly father, help me be present. Be near me during these manic times. Give me the patience so see my child through their healing. Wash over me your Holy Spirit, in your name I pray. Amen.

51. Simply Together

By Brenda Wagenknecht

" But we will arm ourselves for battle[a] and go ahead of the Israelites until we have brought them to their place." (Numbers 32:17 NIV)

We were at a crossroads. We did not know where to turn. We had waited years for local doctors to identify the illnesses our daughter was facing without success. They were even less successful at providing us with help. Time was running out for the homeschooling in a cross-cultural mission setting for our kids as they were approaching adulthood. Our children with special needs had been on a state waiting list for seven years, meaning there was little hope of services until they were nearly 50. . . .

Little did we know that the fever that woke her the morning after her yearly well visit was the beginning of a life-and-death battle. Local doctors could not find the root cause for her symptoms of constant need for sleep, lethargy, inability to eat, and sometimes inability even to lift her head up. Nearly a year passed with only increasing symptoms as she was obviously in a battle to cling to life. As parents we were worried. We prayed for answers. We drove hours to see doctors. We drove across the country to find answers. Nothing made sense. The pit in our stomachs only grew as doctor after doctor threw up their hands and said there was nothing they could find or do. Every test had been run, from MRIs to sleep studies, and bloodwork to EEGs.

My "Mama Bear" research mode, however, would not stop. After spending day and night digging deep into medical journals and connecting with fellow parents across the world whose children had similar symptoms, I found a little-known and difficult to diagnose condition that included brain swelling. Its details kept me reading into the wee hours each night since her symptoms fit with every one of the criteria. The prognosis was not good. There was very little that medical research had found to be successful at reducing the swelling of the brain.

I had cried daily for two years at this point. I had sat on her bedside each day praying that she would be released from her often catatonic state. We knew we could wait no longer. Our daughter needed to be near doctors that had experience with her condition.

Our son had homeschooled his entire elementary and middle school years. While raising our children in remote cross-cultural mission fields provided many blessings, it also brought challenges. We were living in a location that our children would not continue to live in adulthood. During teenage years, world missionaries often send their children back to the parents' home country for school. The main goal: to familiarize with and even acclimate to the parent's home culture before adulthood. This was a dreadful decision for us as adoptive parents—

do we send our child a couple thousand miles away to a culture that was "foreign" to him and a school that did not understand his unique needs? Or do we keep him in a homeschooling situation that he was ready to move on from in a culture where he would not remain into adulthood? Would the experience be one more trauma through which to live?

We brought home our youngest son through adoption at the same time that Steve's ministry had taken us across state lines moving into a cross-cultural setting. The mountains of red tape had taxed our patience as we strove to maintain his foster and adoptive child benefits. We were his second adoption home, and we resolutely said that he would never need a third. Arriving in our new home, we heard the shocking news of the number of children already on the state waiting list. Before he would receive any state services, 54,602 were ahead of him. He was 54,603. The wait began… and years passed till we realized the reality that our son could not receive services that he desperately needed where we were living. No therapies. No respite care. No living assistance when he would turn 18. This was not okay in our minds; we were intent on finding him somewhere to provide a supervised work situation and semi-independent living arrangement rather than being stuck living with his parents as an adult.

Tough decisions lay before us! First, we prayed for answers and asked that the Lord's will be done! We had faced many situations in parenting when we had to make difficult decisions, but this was a crossroad like no other. Steve's ministry did not allow him to choose his work location, and we fully trusted that the Lord would lead us to each next step we needed to take.

I constantly researched. We had daily, prayerful discussions about the path God wanted us to go down. Nothing seemed right. Steve even was called to serve in other ministries. It didn't change our challenges. These potential "new jobs" only brought more potential challenges all their own, plus the stress of a move and adjusting to a new culture.

There was, however, one option that kept creeping back into our list of brainstorm options: buy a home to use as a home base near where our children had already spent many of their childhood years and in a city that had both the potential educational, long-term care options, and medical services we needed. It seemed crazy even to us "out of the box" thinkers! How could we "live" in two locations so far apart? What would the members of our church family think? How could we afford it? How could we maintain our family unity while residing in two locations?

Then God made it clear: How could we not? How could we not put our son in a Christian high school, but have a home nearby for us to visit him often? How could we not get our daughter near doctors that specialized in her condition? How could we not put things in place to provide what our son would need as an adult? Tough decisions were made, but they were always made together as a family.

It started with a home purchase, followed by an establishment of residency for my children and myself. Thankful for hand-me-downs and garage sales, we figured out what to sleep on and eat off in an empty house. Then we found doctors. Then we found schools and programs that would help our children's education and special needs. This all took time—months, years, in fact. It took much more time than we expected.

It was hard. So hard. Steve longed to be with us and help address the difficult life challenges our kids were facing. I longed to have his support in the same house, not just on our twice daily phone calls. The kids missed dad. There were moments when we wondered how we could go on... but we could not go back to a situation where we did not meet our children's basic needs. We leaned on each other, and we moved forward day by day, together.

Through it all, God used our physical separation to shower us with blessings! We learned that physical separation does not divide us as a family, but keeps our bonds tightly wound together. We turned to Him for strength, knowing we could not do this by ourselves. We learned that a family makes sacrifices, really hard ones, when needed. We made it obvious to our children, church, friends, and colleagues that we were not separated because our marriage was in trouble, but we could take such a difficult step because God had blessed us with a strong relationship.

Blessings upon blessings became evident, some we could have never imagined in our wildest dreams. Steve's congregation was very supportive of the children's need for this "apart situation" and allowed for frequent trips to be with the family. Our son had a school environment where other adults shared Jesus with him every day. Another son had an opportunity to play his beloved golf game competitively in high school and succeed. We finally had a doctor who drew seventy vials of blood work to identify the dozen underlying infections that were causing our daughter's brain to swell. We had hope that our youngest would have services as he turned 18. Our marriage grew stronger, not because we were apart, but because we were committed to loving each other even when we were apart.

When the Israelites entered the promised land of Canaan, the men of the tribes who would settle east of the Jordan River made the sacrifice of being apart from their families for a time. In Numbers 32:17 NIV, they told Moses, "But we will arm ourselves for battle and go ahead of the Israelites until we have brought them to their place. Meanwhile our women and children will live in fortified cities, for protection from the inhabitants of the land." As a parent, you never want "somewhere away from you" to be the best place for your family to live.

Reflection

- What difficult situation in your life has God blessed?
- Where can you look for "out of the box" ways to meet the challenges you are currently facing.

Prayer

Dear Lord, You know the challenges that we face each day. Each of us has our own burdens to carry. Help us never forget that You use those trials to bless us by keeping us close and relying on your strength. Help us never give up hope even in the toughest situations and the lowest times. Help us remember that during these times You are bringing us through the turbulence of this world to prepare us for an eternity with You in the mansions of heaven. Amen.

52. Simply Together Forever

By Julie P. Watson

"God decided in advance to adopt us into his own family by bringing us to himself through Jesus Christ. This is what he wanted to do, and it gave him great pleasure."
(Ephesians 1:5 , NLT)

Adoption. Such a beautiful word for so many. Unfortunately, not all share the same feelings. Not every adoption is wanted, especially by older children and teens. They often struggle with the feeling that they are somehow abandoning their biological parents by legally becoming a part of another family. I have heard some sad stories; truly heartbreaking. But, many adoption stories are positive. I will choose to focus on those primarily because adoption was created by God, for His pleasure, through Christ Jesus. It's a beautiful picture of belonging to the One who designed and created us because of His love for those He calls His own.

Going into fostering, my husband and I knew we wanted to adopt. We also knew there were risks of adopting through the foster care system because so many children are not legally free to be adopted. One of my aunts was the first person I knew who fostered children. She had several kids come through her home, and she loved each one as her own. One girl, in particular, had attached to her quite strongly. My aunt and uncle petitioned to adopt her, but her biological father, who wanted nothing to do with her, would not terminate his parental rights. Never mind the fact that he had married a new woman, had children with her, and never wanted to care for this child again. He just didn't want to give up his rights to her. There was nothing anyone could do. Legally, foster parents have no rights over foster children. My aunt was devastated, and this young lady was so broken, she was later moved to a new foster home and eventually ran away. My aunt never knew what happened to her, but over thirty years later, she still thinks about her today.

I did not desire that kind of heartache. I knew there were no guarantees, but having already gone through the heartache of ovarian cancer and infertility, I didn't think I could take much more. When we signed up to become foster/adoptive parents, after hearing about thousands of kids who ARE legally free waiting to be adopted (meaning parental rights were already terminated), we decided to focus on that population. We sought a low-risk placement, meaning a high chance of a successful adoption.

Initially, after we were matched, our children's social worker thought we would be standing in an adoption courtroom finalizing our adoption within nine months. Since all adoptions out of foster care in California require a minimum six months of fostering first, we felt nine months sounded perfect. But oh, how misguided we were! There were many variables I won't get into, but our nine months turned into twenty-one months and ten different social workers. I don't know how typical that is, but we learned from the county where our kids hail from, it's quite the norm. Social workers are overtaxed, and adoption cases only get "fit in" around other, more pressing cases. One social worker from that county actually told us they gave a nickname to the adoption department. Internally, they referred to it as the "dumping ground." I was shocked and horrified! But given the caseload of these social workers, I tried to put myself in their shoes. It still didn't make our situation any easier.

I was tired of fostering. I was so ready to be a real family, and the kids seemed ready too. When we met our children, they had already been legally free for adoption for sixteen months. They were truly waiting children, meaning those waiting on placement into a permanent family. They were the exact population we desired to serve. We greatly hoped to keep a sibling set together. Our three may have been easily separated if left in the system much longer. We were happy to get them out, give them a devoted home and forever family who loved and wanted them!

So, when we finally got the word that our official adoption signing would take place in March 2016 and standing before the judge would happen in April, we were beyond ecstatic! We made plans to celebrate such a special occasion. We had official family portraits done so we could send announcements out and invite everyone to our celebration and child dedication at church on Mother's Day that year (truly one of the top Mother's Days ever).

Simply Dedicated

We made our way to the courthouse that morning, all spiffed up looking our best. We had an early time slot. The air was chilly as we waited for the courthouse to open. We were so thankful to have my parents and older brother join us for this special day. My stomach fluttered with excitement that this day had finally arrived, a mere twenty-one months after our kids walked through our door! We sat down for a bit while waiting for the judge; the bailiff was so sweet and gentle with the kids, giving each a teddy bear. We quickly stood in respect and anticipation when the judge came out to take the bench. She hastily read through some formalities, explained the process, and greeted us on such a special day. After my husband and I swore an oath to care for them just as we would biological children, she explained the court now regarded them as our natural children with all the same rights, requirements, and expectations. My brother recorded it all, and we have an amazing record of it. But nothing made me happier than hearing her welcome the kids into our family, declaring their new legal names. It was so special!

As things mellowed down a few weeks afterward and I reflected, I couldn't thank God enough for carrying us through so many months of difficulties and unknowns. The stress of waiting without knowing anything for months on end nearly broke me. I thought of our kids and all we had gone through, but overwhelming sadness for so many more children in the system who are legally free to be adopted, but won't be. There are too many that age out of the system never knowing the love and commitment of a family.

One fact shared at a foster/adoption conference we attended before ever becoming foster parents has always stuck with me. "If only one family from every church in America took in one foster child, it would wipe out the crisis." Now, that unfortunately wouldn't wipe out the need for foster care going forward, as more kids are being placed in it all the time, but for the kids sitting there now, it would give them a home. That said, not everyone is called to do it, and I respect that. If you're not called, consider helping in various ways those who are called. But, considering you're reading this book, my assumption is you've been called. The Lord will bless what He Himself created. And you can never go wrong when you obey the Lord. Trust Him!

Reflection

If adoption is your desire, and your heart is set on it, please be in constant prayer. The enemy would like nothing more than to steal your peace, kill your hopes, and destroy your faith. But God wants to give you the desires of your heart if it's in His plan for your best life. Adoption was His creation, designed for His pleasure and our future to be with Him forever as royal sons and daughters! What an amazing gift only a loving Father would bestow upon His beloved children! Just be on guard, having faith; not discounting the craftiness of the evil one. God has overcome!

Prayer

Dear Lord, I desire to adopt, but am somewhat trepidatious. Please give me peace and confirm in my heart this desire. I want to be mindful of the importance and huge weight of responsibility it bears, but I also know adoption was Your design. Thank You for creating such a wonderful gift! I want to honor You in all things, especially my home, family, and relationship with You, Lord. Help me to be obedient and answer the call You have placed on my heart, no matter how long and tenuous the journey may be—I am committed! I love You, Father! Amen.

53. Simply Unbelievable

By Tracy Loken Weber

"But as for me, I watch in hope for the Lord, I wait for God my Savior; my God will hear me."
(Micah 7:7, NIV)

It's 4:45 a.m., and the coffee is yet to be brewed. I'm in a deep sleep. And just like that, Bam!!!

She's awake. Our special needs child is A.W.A.K.E!!!

Hyper. Running. Manic. Hitting. Punching. Attacking. LIGHTS ARE ON EVERYWHERE.

As of 4:46 a.m., I knew the day ahead would be one that would keep me running all day long. We've been at this for two years as we remain on waiting lists for professional help to step -in.

Simply Dedicated

Some mornings our daughter wakes up and is peaceful and calm. Unfortunately, more often than not, she wakes up in hysteria, wild, crazy, and uncontrollable. Little did I know what was to come.

Given the first fifteen minutes of the day, I knew we needed to get her professional help when she opened up her window, pushed busted out the window screen, and escaped through her window in -25- degree (Fahrenheit) weather. She was running all around outside in the snow, trying to "escape" from who knows what. My husband opened up the garage door, and she came running in like a wild stallion. I retreated to my home office that is far away from earshot of our other two children and quickly called the local mental hospital from where she was just released from twenty-one 21 days before. In December, she spent sixteen16 days in the mental hospital trying to adjust her medication and stabilization for safety concerns and for her mental health. This was her fifth inpatient hospitalization in one -and -a -half years.

I called the hospital, they pulled up her record, and they could see that we tried to get her admitted a week ago for six straight days. She was recommended for inpatient, but due to no room at the "inn" we continued to plug along. However, given her medical needs for safety and other relevant updates, she was once again, today --- recommended for inpatient. Yet, again, no beds were available at any of the three mental hospitals. The recommendation was to try to keep her safe, and if needed, we were to "call 911" or "take her to the our local emergency room.".

This recommendation statement caused grave concerns for me. I have had have two other children in our home, her siblings who also have post-traumatic stress disorder (PTSD). If the police were to be called, their trauma would be triggered as they are afraid of the police. Any form of a police presence causes their post-traumatic stress disorder to take them back to the moment they were forever removed from their parents. I have seen that fear on their face, and I need to do whatever it takes to remove that fear from their lives. The second statement was to "take her to our local emergency room.". Sure thing, here I have a raging child, who is attacking anyone around her;, how do I get her to the hospital safely as she is attacking me as I drive? She's done it before, attacked me in the car with her shoes, booster seat, you name it, she's used it on me all while driving. --- She will not stay in her seat belt; she is attacking. Taking her here anywhere again is not an option as she's raging.

The mania continued until 10:45 a.m. My husband had to stay home from work because she was is gaining in strength and, power, as she was especially when she's raging. It was 's a non-school day for her siblings, yet she had school. Due to her mania, we kept her home from school and finally at 10:45 a.m. she began to calm down.

Breathe, I told tell myself. Breathe. In…out…in…out… She was exhausted herself. Six hours of hysteria, and she was she's finally tired, calmed down, yet still very hyper alert. I phoned the hospital again, and they had "good news" to share— - the voice on the other end of the phone sounded as if I had just won the Publisher's Clearing House million dollars. This time, the "win" was that after weeks of calling for help, a bed was going to be available at 2 p.m. today. The next question from the hospital staff, was what time could I get there with her?...

Relief. Help was just a few hours away. Now, to quietly get her packed up and to, find someone to come to our home to watch the other kids

Simply Dedicated

(or take them away for a few hours) so my husband could get back to work and I could get her to a safe place where the doctors can perform a medication watch and really truly seek out help for her. We quietly sprang into action, packed her bag, pillow, favorite stuffed animals, markers and paper, and a few coloring books, and my husband took the siblings away from the home as I worked to get her to the hospital.

I knew that if I fed her on the way we would be good, so on the way we stopped by her favorite place and picked up her favorite meal, and she ate it on the way. At age six, she was so smart that she knew just by the way I was headed that we were on our way to the hospital. She said, "Mama, are you taking me to the hospital?" I responded by saying, "Do you think I should?" and she said, "Yes, mama, I need help, and they can help me there—, my meds don't work." In that moment, I wanted to completely break down. My little peanut needed help, knew she needed help, and admitted that the medications just weren't working.

This time, she was in the hospital for one entire month. We had to get it right this time. The doctors had to dig deep, and help this little girl stabilize. She needed stability, our family needed safety and for her to be stable.

It was a long month. Her return home was joyous. Pure joy seeing her siblings, a reunification of hugs, kisses, and love. Many "I missed you's,", "I love you's," and sweet, sweet hugs.

That night I rocked our baby girl to sleep, s. Sang her favorite songs, hummed her lullabies, and for now, she was back and stable. Our "inn" was complete; our baby girl was home.

Reflection

- How can you share the needs of your child with professionals? What does this look like?
- What do you need to do to be more present in their everyday life?

Prayer

Heavenly Father, in times of trial let me lean on You for unwavering grace, peace, love, and understanding. Help me to use my knowledge of my child to advocate fiercely for their needs;, help guide my thoughts, words, and actions. During times of distress pour over me with patience and, understanding, and allow for my entire body to be empowered to understand where my child is coming from, and allow space for healing to occur. In Your Son's name I pray, Amen.

54. Simply Waiting

By Julie P. Watson

"But those who wait on the Lord shall renew their strength; they shall mount up with wings like eagles, they shall run and not be weary, they shall walk and not faint."
(Isaiah 40:31, NKJV)

Waiting is one of my least favorite things in the world to do. Whether it's waiting in line (especially at the Department of Motor Vehicles), waiting for the doctor, or waiting for a red light to change in traffic—I don't care for it one bit! So, one might ask, Why did we wait so long to pursue adoption? Fair question. In my heart, I always wanted to adopt once I knew biological children would not be possible for me. However, I knew if I was going to adopt a sibling set, it would be impossible to give them all the attention they needed if I still had to work outside the home. So, the short answer is, we had to wait until we could afford to live on one income. In my part of the country, that's nearly impossible.

However, God made it possible, after a very long wait. So, it shouldn't have surprised me how much we would have to wait for literally EVERYTHING in the foster care system. It took us six months to get certified, four more before we got our placement, and another twenty-one months before we could legally adopt our three children. Thirty-one months of additional waiting before this dream of nearly seventeen years became a reality. Let me just warn you, this journey is not for the faint of heart! It nearly broke me a half dozen times. I even came down with shingles just over a year into fostering. Waiting can be STRESSFUL!

Waiting becomes the "norm" in foster care. Whether you're waiting to get state medical coverage activated, therapist appointments started, assessments scheduled, dental work completed, prescriptions written or filled, school registration forms submitted, adenoids removed, occupational therapy exercises practiced, or children put to bed—everything takes so much time. I can't tell you how many times I'd have to call back and forth just to get a new ADHD prescription: first, approved by the psychiatrist, then filled by the pharmacy, but only after they verified with the regular doctor, then approved by state medical coverage. That one task alone would often take a few days to complete. Time is an unusable gift to those with more tasks to do than hours in a day.

If you are already a parent, you know how much time it takes for literally everything. Learning how to wait patiently should be a required parenting class. Yet, what is God trying to teach us in the wait? Is there something we need to work on ourselves, come to terms with, or overcome? One thing I learned during my long wait for children is that God's timing is perfect. Had we tried to adopt earlier in our lives,

I would've had to work outside the home, leaving the children in the hands of babysitters or daycare providers. That was not what I wanted. If I was blessed enough to become a mother, I wanted to be present for all of it!

Still, it was a long wait. In 2013, I was 42 years old and starting to feel my age. On Palm Sunday that year I had an intimate, heartfelt talk (and cry) with God reminding Him of my desire to become a mother. My husband and I had talked about it many times over the years, but the finances always kept our plans on hold. This time I prayed with an expectant heart. I wanted an answer, like yesterday. My "deal" with God was that if I didn't have confirmation from Him in my 42nd year, I was going to give up this dream of parenting and start planning a future without children. (Don't you just love the "deals" we make with God? Kind of laughable, really.) God was so precious to me, and He loved me so deeply, He PROFOUNDLY answered my prayer only five days later on Good Friday. I specifically kept my prayer to myself and hadn't shared it with my husband. Yet, while we were home watching TV, not talking about anything at all, out of the blue my husband matter-of-factly said, "I think it's time for us to adopt."

God confirmed it right then and there. My husband and I had not even discussed adoption for over a year. I remember the last discussion in 2012 well. The prospect of it left us feeling defeated, believing adoption was never going to be in our future. Our plans are not His plans, period. Once I shared my prayer and "deal" with my husband, we sat and thanked God for His faithfulness, talked details, and figured out where to start: by sharing the news with our families on Easter Sunday. By proclaiming it to our loved ones, it became very real and strengthened our commitment to our future children. Our children, by the way, were the reason for our wait. They really needed us, and we really needed them. We had to wait for them to be born—thus the wait!

I share this part of my testimony because chances are you've had plenty of experience waiting. Sometimes waiting allows us to deepen our trust in the promises of the Father. He is a good, good Father, always loving, forever faithful. Or, perhaps your waiting is a chance to be refreshed by dipping your toe into the rejuvenating Living Water. Maybe it's simply a time for you to be still in the Lord, casting off all other momentary concerns and just being in His loving presence. Whatever you are waiting for, remember, God may be using this time to reach you in a very unique and special way. Ask Him to reveal the reason for your wait, in His perfect timing, when you are able to understand and be thankful for it.

Reflection

The Lord's ways are so special, so unique, we cannot possibly understand them all. But, rest assured, one day we will know His reasons. I once heard a pastor explain it like this, "We are all players on a football field, but we can see only the play right in front of us. The Lord is like the blimp above—He can see the whole field and every possible play within it—including the best play." That's so true of life. We can only see what's right in front of us. Planning is important, but often a joke! The minute we plan something, "Murphy" (of Murphy's Law), comes along and totally disrupts our plans. But, God sees it all and knows there are times waiting is required so we don't have an interception or fumble on the field. Trust Him!

Prayer

Heavenly Father, You are a good, good Father, and I trust you in all things. I have had to wait for some things that have made me wonder, made me question, and even caused me to doubt. But, You are faithful, and I know there is purpose in the wait. Strengthen me in my areas that are weak. If I need to be still and rest in Your presence, show me how to do that gracefully. Thank You for your perfect timing that keeps my best interest at heart, especially in the wait.

I love You, Lord! Amen.

About The Authors

Simply Dedicated

Tracy Loken Weber, M. Ed.

Tracy has over 25 years of community leadership and service, actively serving on numerous local, state, and international boards. Weber has transformed the educational landscape of both K-12 and adult literacy organizations through the integration of technology and strategic programs. She is currently serving as the State Co-Chair for the Collective Impact Parent Partner for the Wisconsin Office of Children's Mental Health along with Vice-Chair on the Waukesha County Human Services Center Coordinated Service Team and the WELS Foster Care Advisory Group. Tracy is currently serving the UW-Milwaukee Child Welfare Partnership Program as a Foster, Adoptive, and Relative Statewide Trainer.

Weber presents internationally on behalf of adoptive and foster parents, trauma-informed best practices, educational technology and adult literacy issues through associations with the U.S. Department of Education, U.S. Health and Human Services, Wisconsin Office of Health and Human Services, and serves on the Infinitely More Speaker Team.

Weber earned a Bachelor of Science in Education and Master of Science in Curriculum and Design and Instructional Technology and holds a Certificate in Non-profit Management and Accounting. Tracy is also a certified trainer for aha! Process, Inc., in the Bridges out of Poverty Seminars and is trained through the Karyn Purvis Institute of Child Development at TCU in Trust-Based Relationships (TBRI) & Trauma-Informed Classrooms. In August 2020, Tracy became a Master Coach holding Certifications in Professional Life Coaching, Life Purpose Coaching, Goal Success Coaching and Happiness Coaching. She is currently pursuing a Ph.D. in Leadership for the Advancement of Learning and Service at Cardinal Stritch University, expecting to graduate in May 2021.

Tracy and her husband Thomas live in Wisconsin, with their five adopted children.

Connect with Tracy at:
Email: TracyLokenWeber@gmail.com
Website: www.TracyLokenWeber.com
LinkedIn: @TracyLokenWeber
Twitter: @TracyLokenWeber
Blog: https://medium.com/@tracylokenweber
Grab a copy of her books at: https://www.amazon.com/-/e/B08FYYY3XZ

Kim S Bushey, A Fellow Handmaiden

Kim Bushey is a sophisticated homespun, born in Wisconsin, married to Chad for nearly 20 years with 9 adopted children ages 2 through 31. She's got a plethora of testimonies, through valleys and up mountains to share, that will find you wanting more.

A woman who has walked through the many facets of foster care, adoption, loss, trauma, and special needs, Kim Bushey is uniquely qualified to write and speak from the many things God has taught her through the joys and sorrows, the beautiful and heartbreaking. She reminds others that God takes your hand when you feel you can't make it, and the One began a good work completes it.

Writing from authenticity and raw reality, showing the awe-inspiring miracles of God, Kim reminds you that God uses weak things to confound the wise and inspire you to step into bold faith to pursue your calling. Find out more at www.AFellowHandmaiden.com

Erica R. Johnsrud

Erica (Emilson) Johnsrud is an Indiana-born Minnesotan, a devoted wife, and proud adoptive mother of two beautiful, amazingly resilient daughters (soon to be three), and 4 fur babies: 2 cats and two dogs. Erica has been teaching elementary students for well over two decades in a variety of grade levels and positions, but found her true passion was assisting students who struggled with social- emotional and sensory difficulties, brain differences, and/or who were in foster care. As a mother with children with special needs and health issues, she is passionate about helping and supporting these children, other adoptive and foster families, and the families of her students. She personally understands the challenges of raising children with disabilities and complex trauma. Erica is a member of several support groups for families with special needs and a wellness and mental fitness group.

Simply Dedicated

Kirsten Marie Peterson

Born in a small town in Wisconsin, Kirsten demonstrated an extraordinary imagination and knack for storytelling from a young age. She would entertain her brother and dad for hours with her splendid stories of a magical land she lived in and all the antics the eclectic characters experienced. By nature, Kirsten was extremely shy, and these stories were her way of experiencing all that life had to offer, the things she was entirely too introverted to try herself. Although an imaginative child, Kirsten only took pen to paper for school assignments or to write non-fiction reports at home during school vacations.

Having moved from WI to FL in her elementary years, Kirsten had many thoughts, dreams, and stories always swirling in her head but lacked the confidence to share them. Even with several people close to her encouraging her to write them down, Kirsten kept her words tucked safely inside her own mind. Kirsten finally took it upon herself to write a nonfiction magazine article for a local small-town publication and realized the enormous sense of satisfaction she got as a distributor of knowledge.

A teacher for 25 years, Kirsten retired early to homeschool her son. Although this was a successful endeavor for her son's future, she craved to share her knowledge with more than just one student. It was at this time that her love of storytelling for both fiction and nonfiction was reinvigorated. She is currently working on multiple writing projects including a how-to series, a compilation of poems, and more. Kirsten currently resides in Illinois with her 5 children and 2 dogs.

Kisten can be reached at kirstenmariepeterson201@gmail.com.

Simply Dedicated

Karen Schlindwein & Amalie Bowling

Karen Schlindwein
VP of Education/Development of Chosen, Inc.
Co-Author of Dear Lois: Our Adoption Journey

Karen has been married to Tom for 30+ years and lives in Waukesha, Wisconsin. Following an infertility journey that ended in miscarriage in 1991, the couple was connected with Lois, who chose them to be Amalie's adoptive parents. In 1993 Ruth chose them to parent their son, Joseph.

The couple's new-found faith in Christ led Karen to co-facilitate Hope, an infertility/adoption support ministry. She has since been blessed to counsel many through their infertility, adoption and fostering journeys.

Karen recently retired from a 30-year insurance management career in 2015; she then became Chosen's Executive Director at the onset of the ministry. She is now its VP of Education/Development and has the privilege of raising awareness of the great need for more foster/adoptive families and working with many who have a heart and passion for fostering and adoption.

Karen, a foster-sister in her youth, is an adoptive mom to Amalie and Joseph and a grandmother of five, including four through the miracle of adoption. She is a passionate adoption advocate who also enjoys church activities, boating, volunteering at an HIV/Aids organization and, most importantly, family. Karen is a 1986 graduate of Luther College and holds a BA degree in Management. She and daughter, Amalie, are co-authors of Dear Lois: Our Adoption Journey, published in 2015 about their family's adoption experiences.

Amalie Bowling
Chosen, Inc. Co-founder and VP of Outreach
Co-Author of Dear Lois:Our Adoption Journey

Amalie and husband, Jason, married in 2012, and live in Waukesha, Wisconsin. Amalie has a deep passion for adoption and those who are adopted. She and Jason co-founded Chosen, a foster-care and adoption support ministry whose mission is to Foster Forever Families, by living the Gospel, so that all kids can have a safe and loving home

Amalie earned Biblical Studies and Youth Ministry degrees from Emmaus Bible College in 2013 where she was the yearbook design editor and Editor-in-chief. She worked as a claims adjuster for several years and currently as Chosen's VP of Outreach and as an administrative assistant at her local church

In 2015, Amalie and Jason became foster parents. In 2019 the couple adopted four of their foster children (Jayquan, Soraya, Tanaya and Maya) in addition to welcoming Lorelei into their family. Amalie loves to share her adoption story and is passionate about helping foster/adoptive families in their journeys to caring for children in need.

Kevin & Jenny Poston

Kevin and Jenny Poston have been richly blessed with 5 children from age 8 to age 17, and have been foster parents since 2014. They live in Milwaukee, Wisconsin, and are members at Atonement Lutheran Church, where Kevin serves the church and school as Staff Minister of Music, and Jenny serves as Educational Assistant in the Early Childhood Center. Jenny also teaches English online to children in China and crochets unique items to sell in local stores. They enjoy music and other creative activities, family movie nights, coffee and lunch dates, celebrations with extended family, visits from their goddaughter, projects around their home and yard, and caring for their various animals including a small flock of chickens, and enjoying God's creation outdoors.

Brenda & Steven Wagenknecht

Rev. Steven and Brenda Wagenknecht have been married for over 20 years and have raised five children while doing mission work in Latin America and the United States. Steve grew up in a pastor's home in Fort Worth, TX, and graduated from Northwestern College and Wisconsin Lutheran Seminary with a Master's of Divinity. He has been privileged to share God's Word in four Latin American mission fields: Dominican Republic, Mexico, Cuba, and Puerto Rico. Much of his ministry focuses on supporting Spanish speakers, retirement communities, and individuals with special needs.

Brenda grew up on a dairy farm in Zumbrota, MN and graduated with an education degree from Winona State U. After teaching in public and private schools as well as homeschooling her own children, she continued her Master's work at the U. of Arizona in Severe and

Profound Disabilities, as well as adding Master's Certifications in Coaching and Mentoring and Cross-Categorical Special Education. She is a certified HANDLE (Holistic Approach to Neurodevelopment and Learning Efficiency) Screener. Brenda's passion is helping families and private schools meet the needs of students with special needs through her business, Hand and Hand Educational Consulting. She has set up special needs programs in Grenada and Phoenix.

While free time is scarce, Steve and Brenda enjoy spending time with each other, their children and grandchildren, traveling and learning about different cultures, and mentoring parents. They can be either found in Phoenix, AZ where their children reside or in Weslaco, TX where Steve shepherds a congregation.

Simply Dedicated

Julie P. Watson

Aside from being a full-time mother to three beautiful children and wife of 23 years to her loving husband, Julie P. Watson is a published Author, Certified Health Coach and part-time blogger. She is also an ovarian cancer survivor, fear fighter, hope dealer and eternal overcomer! Her story can be found in Made to Overcome: Chronic Illness Edition. While infertility may have been the result of her illness, becoming a mother was still her dream. The journey to motherhood would prove to be a long wait, but when it finally did happen, it came in the form of a "complete family package" -- three children at once. Because of this experience, and all God has brought her through, Julie is a lifelong advocate for children in the foster care system, subsequent adoption out of foster care and pro-life issues all around.

For ten years prior to motherhood, Julie served as an Executive Director, Development Director and Grant Writer for inner-city children's and pro-life ministries. She wrote and won several grants for these ministries. Before ministry, Julie was a Human Resources Generalist for seven years in the corporate world. She holds a Bachelor of Arts in English with an emphasis in Writing and a minor in Biblical Studies from Biola University. She is a member of the San Diego Kingdom Writer's Association (KWA) and facilitates a semi-monthly KWA Writing Critique Group in East County. Praise the Lord, from whom all blessings flow--He has made all things new!

Julie can be reached via email at authorjuliepwatson@gmail.com

Follow her on Facebook at:
www.facebook.com/authorjuliepwatson/

Grab a copy if her books at: amazon.com/author/juliepwatson

Simply Dedicated

Download your free copy of Simply Dedicated Coloring Book at http://bit.ly/SimplyDedicatedColoringBook

Published by Grace & Hope Consulting, LLC

www.graceandhopeconsulting.com

Made in the USA
Las Vegas, NV
23 November 2020